ネイティブの子どもたちも
やっている

音声アプリ&DL対応

英語リプロダクショントレーニング

ビジネス編

改訂新版

小倉慶郎

JN052055

Gakken

音声のご利用方法

方法 1

音声再生アプリで再生する

右の QR コードをスマホなどで読み取るか、下の URL にアクセスしてアプリをダウンロードしてください。ダウンロード後、アプリを起動して『英語リプロダクショントレーニング　ビジネス編　改訂新版』を選択すると、端末に音声がダウンロードできます。

https://gakken-ep.jp/extra/myotomo/

方法 2

MP3 形式の音声で再生する

上記の方法1の URL、もしくは QR コードでページにアクセスし、ページ下方の【語学・検定】から『英語リプロダクショントレーニング　ビジネス編　改訂新版』を選択すると、音声ファイルがダウンロードされます。

ご利用上の注意

お客様のネット環境およびスマホやタブレット端末の環境により、音声の再生やアプリの利用ができない場合、当社は責任を負いかねます。また、スマホやタブレット端末へのアプリのインストール方法など、技術的なお問い合わせにはご対応できません。ご理解いただきますようお願いいたします。

本書は（株）ディーエイチシーより 2013 年に刊行された『英語リプロダクショントレーニング　ビジネス編』の本文の一部を新しい情報に書きなおし、イラストやデザイン等をリニューアルしたものです。

はじめに

ビジネスに即役立つ、社会人向けスピーキング・トレーニング

筆者は現在は大学教員をしていますが、プロ通訳者・翻訳者として活動し、通訳学校ではビジネスパーソンを対象に講師をしていた時期があります。また、現在も企業から英語研修を頼まれることもあります。

ある大手メーカーで、通訳訓練法を使ったビジネス英語スピーキングの研修をした時のことです。学習意欲のある社員 30 人ほどが受講生でした。研修終了後に一人の男性社員が私のところへ来てこう言ったのです。

「自分は英語が苦手です。でも**こういう英語のトレーニングならやってみたい**。今回の研修は１回きりなので、**一人で練習できるいい参考書はありませんか？**」

時間の都合で詳しい事情は聞けませんでしたが、彼は何度も英語の学習で挫折しているようでした。おそらくこう言いたかったのではないでしょうか。「目的のはっきりしない一般英語の学習は、なかなか上達しないし、あまりやる気が起きない。しかし**業務に直結する、ビジネスパーソン向けのスピーキング訓練ならやってみたい**。英語力があまりない人でも取り組め、すぐに効果が上がるものがいい」。

結局、「いい参考書はありませんか？」という問いに対して、私はこう答えるしかありませんでした。「今日使ったテキスト、進め方は私のオリジナルで、同じようなビジネス参考書はないんですよ。これから私がいい参考書を作りますから、それまで待っていてください」。

“世界規模の人材争奪戦” が始まった

私は現在、外国人留学生に通訳・翻訳の実務指導もしています。私の授業を受講する外国人留学生の約半数は、すでに母国語（または英語）と日本語の通訳・翻訳の実務経験があります。帰国後に、自国に進出している日本企業で通訳をする学生もいます。最近は、日本企業が外国人留学生の優秀さを認めて積極的に採用するようになったので、また日本に舞い戻り、日本の企業に就職する学生も増えています。

こうして20年も教えていると、留学生を通じて、世界中の若者の英語力が手に取るようにわかるようになります。世界の大学生の英語力は近年急速に伸びました。もちろん日本の大学生の英語運用力も、昔と比べると向上しましたが、それでも、日本はアジアで一国だけ取り残されているのが現状です。「本書の学習をはじめる前に」(P.12〜) でも触れていますが、アジア各国の若者は、学校の授業だけで、英語で問題なくコミュニケーションする力をつけているのです。

ほぼ全世界規模で、若い世代が、学問・ビジネスの共通語として英語を使う時代になった、といって間違いはありません。そのため世界中の大学・企業で、優秀な人材の争奪戦が始まっています。当然ながら、日本企業も優秀な人材を放っておくわけがありません。最近は日本人大学生が就職後、たった数年で会社を辞めるケースが増え、日本企業は昔と同じように長期的に社員教育をするのが難しくなっています。そこで、即戦力となる優秀な外国人留学生を採用する企業が増えています。また英語を社内公用語にする日本企業もいくつか出てきています。これらは、世界規模で優秀な人材を確保するための必然の流れととらえることができます。すでに日本も“世界規模の人材争奪戦”に巻き込まれようとしているのです。

ビジネス英語スピーキングの画期的入門書

本書は、2024年同時刊行の『英語リプロダクション トレーニング』(以下『英語リプロ』) の姉妹本に当たります。『英語リプロ』では、日本で英語を勉強してきた人が「なぜ英語を話せないか」を明らかにし、通訳訓練法を一般学習者向けにアレンジした、一人でできるスピーキング・トレーニング法を紹介しました。

『英語リプロ』は一般学習者向けに執筆したわけですが、こうした“世界規模の変化”を身近に感じるにつれ、「ビジネスパーソンが“話せるようになった”と実感できる英語のスピーキング・トレーニング本が日本人に必要だ」と思うようになりました。また先ほどの受講生の要望も強く印象に残っていました。そこに、Gakkenからの“ビジネスパーソン向けスピーキング訓練の本を”という依頼を受けて執筆したのが、本書『英語リプロダクショントレーニング　ビジネス編』なのです。

本書は、TOEIC® 500 ～ 600 点以上の英語力の人を対象に、ビジネス英語のスピーキングをどうやったら学べるか、どうしたら業務に直結する英語を身につけることができキャリアアップできるか、という多くの人の疑問に答えたものです。

私が本書執筆にあたって特に心がけたのは以下の 3 点です。

(1) 比較的平易な英語を用いたこと

一般にビジネス英語の参考書は、高度な内容、難しい英語を使ったものが多いようです。ですが実際は、そんな難しい英語を使いこなせる日本人ビジネスパーソンはほとんどいませんし、その必要もありません。簡単な英語でも十分に業務を遂行できるのです。そういう考えから英語はできるだけ平易なレベルにしました。といってもあまりやさしくしてしまうと、「カタコト英語」になってしまうので、TOEIC® 500 ～ 600 点以上の英語力がある読者を想定した、格調のある英語を心がけました。

(2) 応用性（汎用性）の高い厳選されたシチュエーション

次にどの分野のビジネス英語を扱うかです。ビジネス英語と一口にいっても網羅的に扱うと分厚い百科事典のようになってしまい、実用的ではありません。ビジネスのどの分野でも使う可能性があり、応用の利く 20 のシチュエーションに絞りました。本書には 500 以上の重要単語・語句のクイック・レスポンス（詳細は後述）の練習がありますが、これだけでもビジネス英語スピーキングの入門として即効性があると思っています。

(3) “英語を使えるビジネスパーソン” になれる方法を明らかにする

ビジネスで英語を使って活躍している人のほとんどが、海外留学経験があるか、もともと英語が得意であった上に企業の実務で磨かれた人です。「あまり英語を話すのは得意ではない」、「今のところ企業の実務でも英語を使う機会があまりない」というレベルの人にとっては、国際派ビジネスパーソンは「高嶺の花」と思えるかもしれません。しかしビジネス英語入門の人でもやがて頂上にたどり着けるような “道筋” があります。その道筋を「本書の学習をはじめる前に」(P.12 ～) に書きました。

将来グローバルに活躍したい大学生や、入社数年目の社員で今一つどうしたらいいかわからない、という人のために「当たり前」のことを書いたつもりです。すでに第一線で活躍しているビジネスパーソンにとっては「当たり前」のことでも、些細なことでつまずいている人が多いのです。頂上にたどり着くには、さまざまな障害を克服していかなければなりません。たとえば皆さんは次の 4 つの問題をどう克服していますか?

① **グローバル人材の前提となる TOEIC® 800 点以上を取得するにはどうしたらいいのか?(→「まず基本的な英語力を身につけよう」p.22)**
② **そもそも社会人として、経済・ビジネス分野に精通するためにはどうしたらいいのか?(→「基本的なビジネス・経済知識を身につけよう」p.23)**
③ **ビジネスパーソンとして、ライバルに差をつけるには?(→「広く、深く勉強する」p.24)**
④ **本書でビジネス英語の基礎を勉強した後、自分の専門分野の英語(単語・語句)を身につけるにはどうしたらいいのか?(→「フリーランスの通訳者が使う裏ワザ」p.25)**

「本書の学習をはじめる前に」ではこれらの質問に、筆者のビジネス通訳の経験、通訳指導の経験から、わかりやすく回答しています。

プロ通訳者もやっている“話すため”のメソッド

『英語リプロ』でも書いたように、英語を話す力を劇的に向上させるには、1 日に最低 30 分は英語を話す訓練をしなければなりません。といっても、たとえ英語圏へ行っても、努力しなければ 1 日 30 分間英語で話す時間を取ることは困難です。まして日本で、1 日に 30 分間連続で英語を話す練習をすることは、多忙なビジネスパーソンにとっては難しいことでしょう。**しかし、このテキストを使って 1 日 30 分練習すれば、30 分間ずっと、英語を話す効果的なトレーニングができます。1 時間練習すれば、1時間の効果的な話す訓練ができます。なぜなら本書の Step 1～4 の練習は、すべてひたすら口を動かすトレーニングのみだからです。**本書の構成は、かなりの練習量をこなす仕組みとなっているので、とりあえず 3 週間続けていただければ、「口が自然に動く」「話せるようになった」と実感できるはずです。

本書を活用し、皆さんが将来グローバル人材として活躍できることを祈っています。

最後に、素晴らしい編集技術で協力してくれた編集部の皆さん、優れた英文テキストを書いてくれたMalcolm Hendricksさん、本シリーズを通しておしゃれなイラストを描いてくれたHACHHさんに心より感謝を捧げます。

小倉　慶郎

CONTENTS

本書の学習をはじめる前に

英語が世界共通語となる時代

現在、世界の大半の国で、大学生や若い世代のビジネスパーソンが英語を話せるのは当たり前となっています。これはここ 20 年ほどの傾向です。1990 年頃は、ソ連や中国では、外国人と接することができる特別な立場の人しか英語ができませんでした。第二次世界大戦前に日本の統治下にあった韓国や台湾も、戦後かなりの間、実用的な英語ができませんでした。しかし、1990 年前後を境に世界は大きく変わりました。インターネットの登場とほぼ時を同じくして、世界中で若い世代の英語運用能力が急速に伸びてきたのです。

大阪のある高校の先生から聞いた話です。モンゴルからの留学生（高校生）が、あまりに英語が流暢に話せるのでびっくりして、どうしてそんなに英語が話せるのか詰問したというのです。彼は、日本語・日本文化に興味があって 1 年間の交換留学で日本にやってきたわけで、モンゴル人の高校生として特別英語ができるわけではありません。英語圏への留学経験があるわけでもなく、学校の授業だけで英語を習得したのです。そのことを確認して、「やっぱり日本の英語教育はどこかおかしいんじゃないか」とこの先生は頭を抱えていました。

しかし、世界で英語ができる若者はこのモンゴルの留学生に限りません。20 数年前まで、英語が話せるソ連人、中国人は稀でした。しかし、今や旧ソ連圏、ロシアの大学生は驚くほど英語ができるようになり、中国本土の大学生は、今では香港の学生よりも英語が話せるようになっています。もちろん韓国、台湾の大学生も流暢に英語を操れるようになっています。かつて英米の植民地であった、インド、シンガポール、マレーシア、フィリピン、香港などであれば、英語が流暢に話せるのは当たり前でしょう。しかし、その他の地域で若い世代の英語運用能力が急速に伸びているのです。

日本でも最近の大学生の英語運用力は、昔と比べると、かなり上がっています。それでも中国、韓国、インドネシア、タイ、ベトナムといった英米の植民地支配をうけなかった地域と比べても、アジアで一国だけ取り残されているのが現状です。世界的に見ると、イスラム圏とスペイン語圏がやや英語習得が遅れているとはいえますが、ほぼ全世界規模で、若い世代が、学問・ビジネスの共通語として英語を使う時代になった、といって間違いはありません。

世界規模で若者が英語が話せるようになった――そのため世界中の大学で、優秀な学生の争奪戦が始まっています。東京大学で秋入学を試みたり、京都大学では教養科目の講義の半分を英語で行う方針を発表しています。ヨーロッパでは母国語を人一倍誇りにおもうフランスでさえも多くの大学の学部、大学院で英語で授業が行われています。これらはすべて、世界の若い世代への英語の普及とそれに伴う優秀な学生の争奪戦が背景となっている、と考えていいでしょう。もちろんビジネス分野でも、ますます英語が国際共通語として使われているのは言うまでもありません。

とはいっても、アジアの中で急激に英語力を落とした地域もあります。それは香港です。イギリスの植民地として、あれほど英語がうまかった香港人ですが、現在の大学生の英語力は急激に低下しています。昔の香港を知る人には信じられないかもしれません。1997 年の香港の中国返還後、中国政府の意図的な英語つぶしがあったのではないかと勘繰らざるをえません。一方、中国本土では、ここ 20 ~ 30 年の間、大都市を中心に、小学校レベルから集中的な英語教育を行ったもようです。その成果が現在の大学生に現れており、いまの中国（本土）の大学生の英語力は一世代前とはまったく変わりました。近年、香港の大学生自らが「いまは、香港よりも中国本土の大学生の方がよっぽど英語ができるよ」と口を揃えて言うようになりました。

「死語」としての外国語教育

「死語」としての外国語教育。耳慣れない言葉かもしれませんが、教育法としては決して珍しいことではありません。「死語」とは「現在は話されていない言語」という意味です。文献等では読むことができるが、話せない言語を意味します。たとえばヨーロッパでは、古典ラテン語、古典ギリシャ語は、死語として学ばれています。ラテン語を勉強する際に、ヨーロッパ人は驚くほど詳細な文法を勉強していきます。そして自国語への訳読で理解していきます。一方で、発音に関しては、当時のラテン語の発音を忠実に再現しようなどと思ってもいません。イギリス人は英語に近い発音、フランス人はフランス語に近い発音、ドイツ人はドイツ語に近い発音でラテン語を読みます。もちろん、授業はラテン語で行われるわけではなく、それぞれの国の母国語で行われます。

こうして勉強したラテン語は、精密に「読む」ことはできますし、簡単なフレーズ程度ならラテン語で言えるようにはなります。が、決して流暢に話せるようにはなりません。しかも、もしもラテン語を話していた古代ローマ人が現代にタイムスリップして現れたら、「彼らはラテン語らしいものを話しているが、発音が悪くて何を言っているのかよくわからない！」と嘆くことでしょう。

今挙げたヨーロッパ人のラテン語の学び方をまとめると次のようになります。

① 文法を詳細に学び形から理解する
② 訳読で理解する
③ 発音はあまり気にしない
④ 読めることが目標で、流暢に話せるようにはならない
⑤ 自国語で教える

「あれ？　これどこかで聞いたことある！」と思った人もいるでしょう。そうです、これこそ日本の伝統的な外国語教育法なのです。「日本の学校英語をいくら勉強しても実用的な運用能力が身につかない、英語が話せない」と批判される最大の理由は、日本が「死語としての外国語教育法」を“無意識に”採用してきたからなのです。

「死語としての外国語教育」の利点

最近は評判が悪い、死語としての外国語教育ですが、もちろん利点もあります。

何よりも、外国語を話す必要がない環境で、辞書さえあれば効果的に文献から知識を吸収できる、ということです。この教育法は日本の近代化に大きく貢献したことは間違いありません。たとえば、近代自然科学はヨーロッパが発祥地です。そのため中心地である西ヨーロッパ諸国やその移民を多く受け入れている国がノーベル賞の自然科学部門（物理学賞、化学賞、医学生理学賞）で圧倒的に優位に立っています。アメリカ、イギリス、ドイツ、フランスなどです。しかしアジア、オセアニア地区だけを見ると、日本が断トツに自然科学部門の受賞数で優位に立っています。これほどの成果は、ヨーロッパ系以外では例外的です。幕末の開国から 170 年の小国が、このレベルに達したことは恐しいこととさえいえます。この日本の急速な西洋化、近代化の一つの軸になったのが「死語としての外国語教育」であったことは忘れてはなりません。短期間で西洋の文献を読み吸収するには、話す・聞くといった実用運用能力を犠牲にしたこの方法が一番効率的だったのです。それは日本のエリートたちへの教育として最も効果的でした。その後、海外留学などで実用的な運用能力を身につける必要に迫られた人たちも、詳細な文法力と読解力をもとに、——もちろんかなりの努力は必要でしたが——短期間で実用外国語（英語）を身につけられたのです。

◢ 制度疲労を起こした英語教育

こうして日本が世界の一流国の仲間入りをするのに大いに貢献した伝統的外国語教育法ですが、急速なグローバル化と実用的な英語運用能力の緊急の必要性のもと、ついに終焉を迎えようとしています。なぜなら伝統的な英語教育をいくらやっても、話し、聞くことのできる実用的な力が身につかないからです。実用的な英語力を習得するためには、発想を転換し勉強方法を変えなければなりません。英語がビジネス・学問の共通語となり、世界の若い世代にとって必須なコミュニケーションツールとなった今、「使える英語」の習得が急務となっています。

こうした現状を知り実感している日本人は、いまのところビジネス、学問の第一線で活躍している一部の人に限られます。しかし、その人たちを中心に日本の英語教育の改革が叫ばれ、日本の学校教育も大きく変わろうとしています。

小学校での英語教育導入、中学・高校では英語で授業をすることを基本とする新学習指導要領の導入、大学・大学院入試におけるTOEFL®の利用――これらはすべて、「世界で取り残されつつある日本の英語教育を早急に改革しなければ」という現状をよく知る人たちからの要請がもとになっていると考えられます。

英語を話せるようになるには

グローバルに活躍しているビジネスパーソンを見ると、以下の2つのケースに大きく分類できるようです。

① 日本だけで英語を勉強したが、企業で英語を使うことを必然的に求められ、現場で英語力を培ってきたケース。
② 留学で英語力を身につけ、それをもとに現場の英語力を身につけたケース。

この両方のケースの共通項は、「英語漬け」を経験したことです。学校教育の分野では「英語イマージョン」という言い方もします。会社の仕事もプライベートの会話もすべて英語にしてしまえば、必然的に実用的な英語運用能力が身につきます。事実、社内公用語を英語にした企業もありますが、これは「英語漬け」で使える英語を習得しようという考えから来ています。海外留学でMBA取得などを目指せば、これも効果的な英語イマージョンになります。しかし、平均的なサラリーマンには、こんなことはお金と時間の制約もあり難しいのではないでしょうか。

先ほど説明したとおり、私たちの英語学習法は「死語」としての外国語教育で、話すことを完全に無視した教育法でした。したがって皆さんが英語を話せないとしたら当然の結果といえます。逆に日本式英語教育を受けながら英語を流暢に話せるのであれば、何らかの特別な努力を払った結果です。問題はどうしたら日本の伝統的教育で培った英語力を、留学や英語イマージョンなど「英語漬け」のない環境で、使える英語力に転化できるか、です。

まずはっきりさせたいのは、学生時代「死語」としての学習で培った文法力、語彙力、読解力は無駄ではなかったということです。この力はまだ“眠った状態”で皆さんの中にあります。この力を使える状態に変えることが必要です。この眠った力を呼び起こし、短期間で英語運用能力を実用レベルまで高めるトレーニングこそ、私が現在普及に力を注いでいる「通訳訓練法」なのです。このトレーニングによって、今まで一見役に立たなかった「眠っている力」が目を覚まし、実用的な英語運用能力が著しく改善されると考えられます（図1）。

■［図1］訓練とその効果①

「通訳訓練法」とは？

「通訳訓練法」とは、インタースクールを中心とする日本の通訳学校で開発された日本人向けの実用的英語学習法と考えてください。シャドーイングが一番有名です。「開発された」というと一定の意図をもって考案したように思えますが、実情は違うようです。日本で英語教育を受けた日本人受講生を、“使える英語”を駆使するプロ通訳者にするためにはどうしたらいいのか——。そのために、通訳学校が長年試行錯誤し、さまざまな練習法の中で最終的に生き残ったのが一連の通訳訓練法である、と私は考えています（「日本人学習者向けのシャドーイング」が生まれた経緯については『英語リプロダクション トレーニング　入門編』に書きましたのでぜひお読みください）。

私もかつては通訳学校の受講生の一人で、30歳を目前にしてスクールの門戸を叩きました。その後プロ通訳、翻訳の実務を経て、現在は大学教員が本業です。

もともと通訳訓練は英語能力が高い受講生（たとえばTOEIC® 900点以上）を対象にしています。それを何とか一般学習者向けにわかりやすくアレンジできないか、と私は考えてきました。そして、ついに完成したのが「英語リプロダクショントレーニング」です。これは、一般英語学習者にも効果のある通訳訓練法として、クイック・レスポンス、シャドーイング、リピーティング注1、日→英サイト・トランスレーションを取り入れ、最後にイラストを使った英語による説明練習でスピーキングの実力を完成させる、という練習法です。本書ではこの一連の練習を「英語リプロダクション トレーニング」と呼びます。一人で気軽にできるスピーキング練習法として、好評を得ています。

注1：通訳学校では長めのリピーティング練習を行い、それをリプロダクションと呼ぶのが普通です。

◪「翻訳語彙」を転換しなければコミュニケーションができない

通訳訓練法でなぜ話せるようになるのか、もう少し分析的に考えてみましょう。通訳訓練法はもともと「通訳者養成のためのトレーニング」で、英語を話すことに特化したトレーニングではありません。しかし、その中でもクイック・レスポンス、シャドーイング、リピーティング、日→英サイト・トランスレーションの４つは、話す力の養成に深く関連していると考えられます。その種明かしは、語彙レベルで考えるとよくわかります。

通常、死語としての学習法で勉強してきた人は、英語を日本語に「翻訳」しないと意味が理解できません。ここで「翻訳する」というのは、文字で書かなくても、頭の中で日本語に転換するという意味です。今の大学生も、特に予備校で死語としての学習で集中的に勉強した場合、日本語に訳さないと英語が理解できないケースが見受けられます。訳さないと理解できない語彙――これこそが学校英語から実用英語運用能力への転化を妨害する元凶です（日本の英語教育は文法をやるからダメだなどとピント外れのことを言う教育者がいますが、文法を学習しないと外国語をきちんとマスターすることは絶対にできません）。この語彙は、説明的に「翻訳転換理解語彙」と呼ぶのが一番いいのですが、長いので略して「翻訳語彙」と呼ぶことにしましょう。

なぜこの語彙が元凶なのかというと、リスニングをすればすぐにわかります。リスニングをすると、どんどん音が流れていくので、訳している暇がありません。したがって「翻訳語彙」のままでは相手の言っていることが全くわからないのです。話すときも日本語から英語へ訳しているとテンポが遅れるので、スムーズな会話が成り立ちません。つまり翻訳語彙のままではコミュニケーションがほとんど成り立たない、ということになります。現在、40歳以上で日本の学校教育だけで英語を勉強してきた人は、ほとんどが翻訳語彙しかないはずです。ですから英語で簡単なコミュニケーションすらできないのが普通です。これが「日本人は中学・高校で6年間、大学も含めると10年近く英語を勉強してきたのに、英語で話せない」という現象の正体なのです。

しかし2006年に日本の英語教育に変化が起こりました。センター試験に英語リスニングが導入されたのです。そのため2006年入学以降の大学生はリスニングが年々できるようになりました。そして2021年からは共通テストが導入されリスニングの配点が50%となり、ますますこの傾向は強まっています。リスニングができるということは、上述したように「翻訳語彙」が別の種類の語彙に変化したことを意味します。翻訳しなくても聞けばわかる、しかし話せない状態の語彙――。これを語学教育の分野ではpassive vocabulary[注2]と呼んでいます。英語リスニングがセンター試験に導入されたために、高校の英語授業や予備校ですらもリスニングを重視するようになりました。「死語」として英語を学習している状態は依然として変わりませんが、繰り返しリスニングをしていると、訳さないでも理解できる語彙（passive vocabulary）が増えていきます。こうして現在の若い日本人の平均的な英語レベルは、全くコミュニケーションができない「翻訳語彙」のレベルから、聞けばわかるpassive vocabularyのレベルに移行しようとしています。

最近は「聞くだけで英語ができるようになる！」という謳い文句の教材が出回っています。英語教育の専門家は「聞くだけで英語ができるようになるわけがない」と口を揃えて言いますが、いままで話したことから、全くウソというわけではない、ということがわかるでしょう。日本で死語としての英語学習をしてきた人が、繰り返しやさしいリスニングをすることによって「翻訳語彙」がpassive vocabularyに変わり、コミュニケーションができる準備段階に達するわけです。

英語で話す機会のある少数の人は、さらに話せる語彙（active vocabulary[注3]）に転換させ、「英語が話せる」ようになる可能性があります。いずれにせよ全く使えなかった語彙が、コミュニケーションに役立つようになるため、現在の日本ではリスニング教材が非常に流行っていると考えられます。しかし、従来型の学習＋リスニングだけでは不十分なのは明らかです。そこから active vocabulary に転換する手立てがないからです。

注 2、注 3：通常 passive vocabulary は聞いたり、読んだりしたら理解できるが、話したり、書いたりはできない語彙を指します。そして active vocabulary は話し、書ける語彙を言います。しかしここでは話をわかりやすくするために、passive vocabulary は「聞いて理解できる語彙」、active vocabulary は「話せる語彙」としています。

翻訳語彙を「使える語彙」に変えるには

以下の図 2 を見るとわかりやすいでしょう。日本人大学生の平均的な英語力の現状は、語彙レベルでみると、現在「翻訳語彙」から passive vocabulary に移行しているところです。普通はイマージョン教育など特別な教育を受けない限り、日本では話せる語彙は簡単には身につきません。

■ [図 2] 翻訳語彙から使える語彙への転移

翻訳語彙 ➡ passive vocabulary ➡ active vocabulary

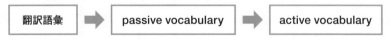

通訳訓練校が採用してきた一連のトレーニングには、翻訳語彙を passive / active vocabulary へと速やかに変化させる訓練法が含まれています。本書で使用するクイック・レスポンス、シャドーイング、リピーティング、日→英サイト・トランスレーションの効果は次のようなものであると考えられます。

■ [図 3] 訓練とその効果②

訓練法の名前	訓練の内容	効果
クイック・レスポンス STEP 1	日本語を見て、瞬時に英単語・フレーズを口で言えるようにする練習	単語・フレーズ単位ですぐに英語を口に出せるようになる→単語・フレーズ単位で、翻訳語彙を active vocabulary に変える。
シャドーイング STEP 2	英語の音声を聞きながら、音声に沿って口まねする練習	発音やイントネーションが改善する。英文を、日本語を介さずに理解できるようになる→翻訳語彙を passive vocabulary に変える。
リピーティング STEP 3	英語の音声を聞いたあとに、それを口で再現する練習	意味のかたまりの単位で、英語を口に出せるようになる→より大きい単位で active vocabulary に変える。
日→英サイト・トランスレーション STEP 4	日本語を見ながら、どんどん英語に訳していく練習	文単位で英語を口に出し、話せるようになる→文単位で active vocabulary に変える。

これは、最初に述べた「図 1：訓練とその効果①」を語彙レベルで分析的に示したものです。このように通訳訓練法によって “眠っていた力” が、“顕在的な力” に転化されるので、著しい効果があるように見えるのです。もちろん翻訳語彙がない場合も、このトレーニングによってはじめから active vocabulary を作ることができます。またこの練習に慣れてくると、知らない単語・フレーズを数回口で唱えただけで、active vocabulary にできるようになり、劇的に実用英語能力が向上することになるのです。

では、通訳トレーニングの話はここまでにして、次節から「使えるビジネス英語」の学び方について考えてみましょう。

まず基本的な英語力を身につけよう

これからビジネス英語を勉強しようとする皆さんに、ビジネス英語を身につける前提条件についてお話ししましょう。

本書は、TOEIC® 500 ~ 600 点以上の読者を対象にしていますが、英語の運用力はできるだけ高い方がいいのです。私の本務校（大阪公立大学）では、TOEIC® 300 ~ 500 点の学生には、インターネットで聞ける NHK の語学番組を毎日 2 番組聞き、できればシャドーイング、日→英サイト・トランスレーションをするように指導しています。さらに TOEIC® 500 点後半～ 600 点以上の学生には、英語のニュース番組を毎日聞くように指導しています。英語ニュースの利点は、毎日違う内容が配信され、さまざまな分野の語彙が身につけられることです。今日は政治のニュースばかりでも、しばらくすると台風や地震のニュースが中心になるかもしれません。来週は経済ニュースが話題をさらうかもしれません。そうして 2 年も聞き続ければ、語彙が 1 万語近くになり、TOEIC® 900 点以上、英検 1 級を狙える語彙力が身につきます。

現在、大学生に人気があるのは、インターネットで見られる NHK WORLD-JAPAN です。日本、アジア、世界のニュースだけでなく、ビジネス・テクノロジー関係のニュースも常時配信しています。このサイトの良いところは、ニュースビデオの下にサマリーが英語で表示されていることです。英語ニュースで挫折するのは、「聞こうとしてもわからないのでやめてしまう」というパターンが一番多いのです。しかし、最初に目でサマリーを読んで、わからない単語・語句を辞書で確認してから英語ニュースを聞くことにより、この挫折パターンを防ぐことができます。この「読む→聞く」という順番が最初は大切で、この順番を守らないとたいてい挫折します。また忙しい人にはスマホのアプリが用意されています。

ですから、パソコンの前に座らなくても、通勤時間を利用して勉強ができます。そして、半年も毎日聞けば英語ニュースを「なんとなく理解できる」レベルに達します。その時点でTOEIC® 800点の実力があることが、今までの学生の指導からわかっています。私が大学生に試した限りでは、このやり方がTOEIC® 800点への最短距離です。ビジネス英語といってもやはり「英語」なので、英語の運用能力は少しでも上げるよう努力しましょう。

基本的なビジネス・経済知識を身につけよう

ビジネス英語の前提の話を続けます。

私は、ビジネスパーソンとして英語を使うよりも、プロ通訳者としてさまざまなビジネス英語を使う状況に直面してきました。通訳者は、他人が話す言語を瞬時に別の言語に変換するわけですから、ただ単に英語を話すよりも、はるかにハードルが高いことは確かです。これから私が通訳者時代に心がけてきたこと、通訳学校の講師として受講生を指導してきたことを中心にお話ししましょう。

まずあらゆる種類のビジネス英語に対応するためには、基本的なビジネス・経済の知識が必須です。プロ通訳者は少なくとも「日本経済新聞」を毎日読んでいます。現在では、ペーパー版でなくとも、インターネットで手軽に読めます。また、同じサイトで同時に英語版も読むことができます。読んでも内容がわからないところが出てくる場合、日経関連の書籍(「日経文庫」など)を数冊は読むといいでしょう。あるいはインターネットで解説記事を探して読んでも構いません。

そのほか「東洋経済」「ダイヤモンド」など面白くてためになる経済記事がインターネットでも読めます。私は「日経ビジネス」を長い間愛読していました。日本経済新聞を中心にそれらも活用していくといいでしょう。

こうした勉強は、ビジネス英語を始める前の基礎中の基礎です。インターネットで日経の日本語版と英語版を毎日読めば、短期間にビジネス全般の知識、基本的な言い回しが日本語と英語で身につくはずです。世の中には「英語ができる」と称する人で「ただし、ビジネス・経済英語はよくわからない」という人も結構多いのです。しかし、こんなに簡単に基本が身につけられるのですから、もしも経済英語に苦手意識があるのなら、大急ぎで基礎固めしましょう。

私の通訳修業時代には、さらに経済学の基礎を固めるために、分厚い入門書を読み進める「勉強会」を主宰していました。毎週土曜日に集まって仲間たちと経済本を勉強したわけです。その中には、今でも基礎がわかると人気のある『ゼミナール日本経済入門』『ゼミナール国際経済入門』(いずれも日本経済新聞出版社）も含まれていました。「勉強会」の主宰者である私は、他のメンバーよりも勉強しなくてはならない立場だったので、予習が大変でした。しかしこうした勉強が、私の経済、ビジネス知識の基礎を作ってくれたことは間違いありません。

「広く、深く」勉強する

通訳修業時代に、先輩通訳者から次のようなアドバイスを受けたことがあります。フリーランス通訳として今後活躍するには…

① 一般的な知識なら、知らないことがないようにしなさい。(当時は「イミダス[注4]人間になりなさい！」と言われました)
② 自分の専門分野を少なくとも３つ作りなさい。また、ある分野の通訳をやったら、関連書籍を何冊か読みなさい。

①は、明日まったく知らない分野の通訳をしなくてはならない場合でも、基本的な知識があれば通訳の準備ができる。だから、普段から少しでも幅広い分野の知識を身につけなさい、という意味です。私は「こりゃ大変だ」と思いながらも「イミダス人間」を目指しました。そして②のアドバイスに従って、私は「経営」「金融」「環境問題」の３分野を自分の専門分野と決め、この３分野については日本語と英語の書籍、文献等をできるだけ読もうと決め実行しました。これは、これからグローバルに活躍しようと考えている皆さんにも、お勧めできる勉強法です。できるだけ広い知識を身につけること（他の人と話題、着想が違ってきます）と専門分野をより深く勉強すること。この２つをしばらく続けてみませんか？

専門分野についてもう少し突っ込んでお話ししましょう。ビジネスの専門実務に関しては、ほとんどすべての人が仕事の中で知識を身につけています。就職してから数年間真面目に仕事をしていれば、業務の中で自然に身につくのが普通です。また会社もその方向で社員を指導してくれるはずです。しかし、私はそれだけでは不十分だと考えています。金融業にいるのなら金融のこと、自動車業界にいるのなら自動車に関連して、仕事で必要とされる以上の勉強を自らに課していくことが大切だと私は思っています。若い人は特に「休日は休養だ」と考えるのも無理はありませんが、休日や平日の退社後の時間こそ、その3分の1、いや4分の1でもいいから自分の勉強のために使わなければなりません。そうしてはじめて、数多くのビジネスパーソンの中で輝くことができるのです。この「広く、深く」という勉強法は、通訳者をやめた今でも私が続けていることです。

注4：『イミダス』とは、かつて集英社が刊行していた現代用語辞典のこと。

フリーランスの通訳者が使う裏ワザ

最後に通訳者が使う究極の裏ワザ、ワードリストとクイック・レスポンスについてお話をしましょう。

本書のレッスンは、「ビジネス全般で使う基本的な言い回しに慣れる」ことを目標にしました。したがってビジネスの各分野で出て来るさまざまな専門用語まで網羅はしていません。もしも各分野の専門用語まで網羅しようとすると「百科事典」のような参考書ができてしまい、研究には役に立つかもしれないが実際には役立たない、ということになるかもしれないからです。しかし、そうは言っても、自分の業務に必要な専門用語を覚えないと本当にビジネスには役に立たない、と考える人は多いのではないでしょうか。

実は、このような専門用語の暗記は、常に通訳者がやっていることなのです。特にフリーランス通訳者は、その分野の専門家ではないのに、専門家同士の通訳をする必要に迫られます。だいたいの基礎知識は事前に勉強できますし、親切な担当者であれば事前にいろいろと質問することも可能です。しかし、問題は専門用語です。専門用語や専門の言い回しを知らなければきちんと通訳できないことが多いのです。もちろん企業内通訳のように、同じ分野の通訳を続けていればその分野の専門用語に精通してくるので問題はありません。問題は、フリーランスの通訳者が、自分の得意でない分野の通訳をするときです。明日頼まれた通訳の分野には、自分の知らない専門用語が数百もあるかもしれません。

そんな時に活躍するのが、ワードリストとクイック・レスポンスです。これらを使って専門用語の部分を切り抜けるのが「通訳者の裏ワザ」です。これは通訳者でなくとも、ビジネスマンが業務に必要な用語を手っ取り早く覚えるのにも役に立ちます。

ここで通訳者が愛用している“ワードリスト”の作り方を説明しましょう。ワードリストといっても単語だけでなくフレーズや短文を載せても構いません。要は自分の専門業務に必要な用語をリストにし、それをクイック・レスポンス（詳しい練習法は後述）で覚えるというだけです。クイック・レスポンスで覚えた単語・語句・文は、active vocabulary に転換されているので、“すぐに使える状態”でスタンバイできるわけです。

フリーランス通訳者がワードリスト作成のためによく使うのが『ジャンル別 トレンド日米表現辞典』（小学館）です。これは通訳学校でも使用されており、経済、政治、法律、社会問題などのジャンル別の現代用語１万８千項目が収録されています。そしてそれぞれの項目に日本語とその英訳、よく使われるフレーズ・例文が掲載されています。試しに『トレンド』（第４版）の、「流通・物流」から日本語と英語の表現を抜き出してワードリストを作ってみましょう。（以下 p. 291 ～ 293 から引用）

流通、物流	distribution
流通業	distribution industry
流通機構	distribution channel [network; system]
流通機構の簡素化が必要とされる。	It is necessary to simplify [streamline] the distribution system.
流通革命	distribution revolution
流通在庫	distribution inventory
流通経路	channel of distribution; sales chain [channel]; distribution channels
物流センター	distribution center
物流部門	distribution arm
市場調査	market research
市場占有率、シェア	market share
会社は鉄鋼市場に 30% の占有率を持っている。	The company has a 30% share of the steel market. / The company shares 30% of the steel market.
独占市場	monopoly market
独占は有効な競争をなくす。	Monopoly kills effective competition.
寡占市場	oligopoly market
新規参入	new entry
参入障害	entry barrier
カルテル	cartel
カルテル行為	cartel activity
やみカルテル	unauthorized [unlicensed] cartel
販売網	sales network [channel, organization]
よくできた販売網	well-organized sales network
役に立たない販売網	useless sales network / sales network that does not work
工場出荷	factory shipment
工場出荷が増加し、まもなく卸売段階でも出荷増があった。	Factory shipments increased, soon followed by another increase of shipments at a wholesale level.
宅配便	home [door-to-door] delivery service; courier service
(宅配便の) 荷物	(home-delivered) parcel [package]
翌日配達・翌日配送	next-day delivery; overnight delivery

このワードリストは、『トレンド』から引用しただけですが、この表現辞典を参考に、その他の資料の用語を加えて自分なりのワードリストを作っている通訳者は数多くいます。また、さまざまなウェブサイトを活用してリストを作ることもできます。みなさんもぜひ自分用の業務ワードリストを作り、クイック・レスポンスで覚えてビジネスに活用してください。必ず役に立つはずです。

それでは、前置きが長くなりましたが、いよいよ次ページからは具体的な本書の学習の仕方を解説します！

本書の使い方

本書には、計 20 レッスンが掲載されています。

- 各 Lesson とも、STEP 1 ～ 4 の 4 ステップ（8 ページ）構成です。
- STEP1 ～ 4 の順に学習を進めます。
- どのレッスンから始めても、また途中のレッスンをとばしても問題ありませんが、まずは Lesson 1 から順番に学習することをお勧めします。

STEP 1 Quick Response　10～30 分

クイック・レスポンス

GOAL 左側の日本語だけを見て、（隠した）右側の英語を瞬時に口で言えるようになる。

この音声トラックを再生して行います

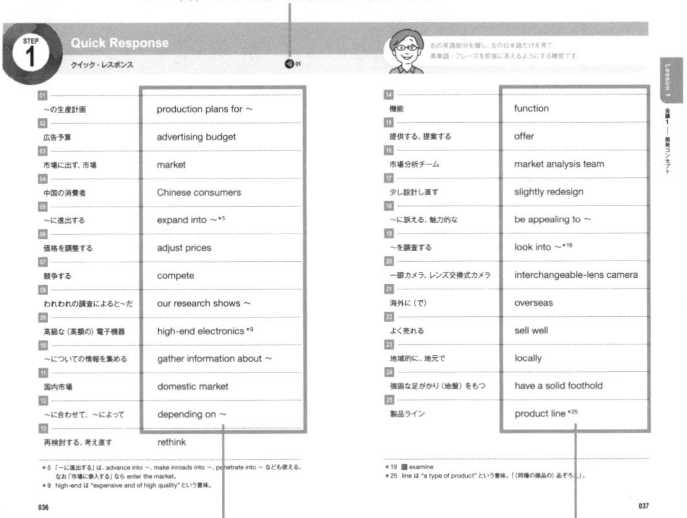
STEP 1 Quick Response
クイック・レスポンス
01
右の英語部分を隠し、左の日本語だけを見て
英単語・フレーズを即座に言えるようにする練習です。

01 ～の生産計画	production plans for ～	14 機能	function
02 広告予算	advertising budget	15 提供する、提案する	offer
03 市場に出す、市場	market	16 市場分析チーム	market analysis team
04 中国の消費者	Chinese consumers	17 少し設計し直す	slightly redesign
05 ～に進出する	expand into ～ *5	18 ～に訴える、魅力的な	be appealing to ～
06 価格を調整する	adjust prices	19 ～を調査する	look into ～ *19
07 競争する	compete	20 一眼カメラ、レンズ交換式カメラ	interchangeable-lens camera
08 われわれの調査によると～だ	our research shows ～	21 海外に（で）	overseas
09 高級な（高額の）電子機器	high-end electronics *9	22 よく売れる	sell well
10 ～についての情報を集める	gather information about ～	23 地域的に、地元で	locally
11 国内市場	domestic market	24 強固な足がかり（地盤）をもつ	have a solid foothold
12 ～に合わせて、～によって	depending on ～	25 製品ライン	product line *25
13 再検討する、考え直す	rethink		

*5「～に進出する」は、advance into ～、make inroads into ～、penetrate into ～ なども使える。なお「市場に参入する」なら enter the market。
*9 high-end は "expensive and of high quality" という意味。
*19 examine
*25 line は "a type of product" という意味。「（同種の商品の）品ぞろえ」。

036　037

Lesson 1　会議 1 ― 開発コンセプト

ここを手などで隠す

1 まずテキストを見ながら、音声に続いて英語を1回ずつ発音します。音声を真似るように心がけてください。

2 まずテキストを見ながら、音声に続いて英語を3回ずつ発音します。音声を真似るように心がけてください。

例

音声　**「production plans for」**

あなた　**「production plans for」「production plans for」「production plans for」**

覚えにくい単語（フレーズ）の場合、3回に限らず何度練習してもかまいません。

3 次に、右側の英語を手などで隠し、最初の単語・フレーズから順番に日本語だけを見て、瞬時に英語で言えるように練習します。上から順番に言えるようになったら、今度は逆の順番でも練習してみましょう。日本語を見て、瞬時に英語が口から出てくるようになったら、STEP 2に進んでください。

いつも間違えるところや覚えにくいところは、赤ペンやマーカーなどでチェックして、集中的に練習するのがコツです。できなければ、何度でも繰り返しましょう。

STEP 2 Shadowing & Repeating　10～30分

シャドーイング&リピーティング

GOAL ［シャドーイング］

テキストを見ずに、英語の音声だけを聞いて口真似できるようになる。

GOAL ［リピーティング］

テキストを見ずに、ポーズのところで、口に出して英語を繰り返すことができるようになる。

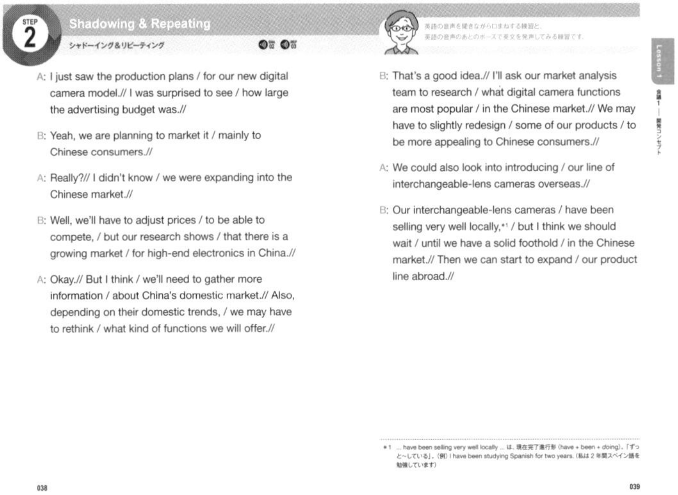

STEP 2 Shadowing & Repeating

シャドーイング＆リピーティング SHA 02 REP 03

英語の音声を聞きながら口まねする練習と、
英語の音声のあとのポーズで英文を発声してみる練習です。

A: I just saw the production plans / for our new digital camera model.// I was surprised to see / how large the advertising budget was.//

B: Yeah, we are planning to market it / mainly to Chinese consumers.//

A: Really?// I didn't know / we were expanding into the Chinese market.//

B: Well, we'll have to adjust prices / to be able to compete, / but our research shows / that there is a growing market / for high-end electronics in China.//

A: Okay.// But I think / we'll need to gather more information / about China's domestic market.// Also, depending on their domestic trends, / we may have to rethink / what kind of functions we will offer.//

B: That's a good idea.// I'll ask our market analysis team to research / what digital camera functions are most popular / in the Chinese market.// We may have to slightly redesign / some of our products / to be more appealing to Chinese consumers.//

A: We could also look into introducing / our line of interchangeable-lens cameras overseas.//

B: Our interchangeable-lens cameras / have been selling very well locally,*1 / but I think we should wait / until we have a solid foothold / in the Chinese market.// Then we can start to expand / our product line abroad.//

Lesson 1 会議1 ― 開発コンセプト

＊1 ... have been selling very well locally ... は、現在完了進行形（have + been + doing）。「ずっと～している」。（例）I have been studying Spanish for two years.（私は2年間スペイン語を勉強しています）

038 039

■ シャドーイング SHA 02 の音声トラックを再生して行います。

1 shadow は「影」。shadowing とは「影」のようについていく、という意味です。最初はテキストを見ながら、音声から聞こえた通りにほぼ同時に口真似していきます。英語を聞きながら話す練習です。

例

音声 **I just saw the production plans for our new digital camera model.**

あなた **I just saw the production plans for our new digital camera model. …**

2 もう一度音声を再生します。今度はなるべくテキストを見ないで行いましょう。

3 すらすらと口が動くようになるまで、何度か繰り返しましょう。まったくテキストを見ないで、すべてシャドーイングできるようになったら、リピーティングに進んでください。

■リピーティング　REP 03 の音声トラックを再生して行います。

1　音声には、テキストのスラッシュ（/もしくは//）ごとにポーズが入っています。このポーズのところで、直前に聞こえた英語を繰り返し発音する練習です。

例

音声　**I just saw the production plans...**

あなた　**I just saw the production plans...**

2　まったくテキストを見ないで、すべてリピーティングできるようになれば合格です！

次からは音声を使わずに練習します。

STEP 3 Sight Translation　10～30分

サイト・トランスレーション

GOAL　左ページの日本語だけを見て、（隠した）右ページの英語を瞬時に口で言えるようになる。

ここを手などで隠す

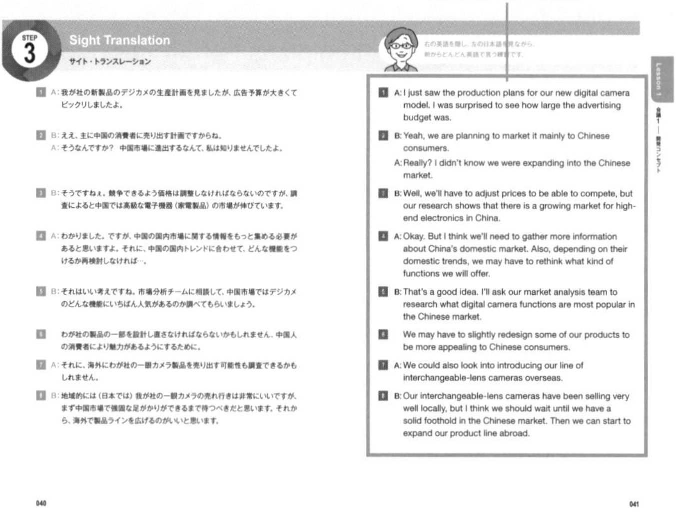

STEP 3 Sight Translation

サイト・トランスレーション

1 A：我が社の新製品のデジカメの生産計画を見ましたが、広告予算が大きくてビックリしましたよ。

2 B：ええ、主に中国の消費者に売り出す計画ですからね。
A：そうなんですか？　中国市場に進出するなんて、私は知りませんでしたよ。

3 B：そうですねぇ。競争できるよう価格は調整しなければならないのですが、調査によると中国では高級な電子機器（家電製品）の市場が伸びています。

4 A：わかりました。ですが、中国の国内市場に関する情報をもっと集める必要があると思いますよ。それに、中国の国内トレンドに合わせて、どんな機能をつけるか再検討しなければ…。

5 B：それはいい考えですね。市場分析チームに相談して、中国市場ではデジカメのどんな機能にいちばん人気があるのか調べてもらいましょう。

6 わが社の製品の一部を設計し直さなければならないかもしれません。中国人の消費者により魅力があるようにするために。

7 A：それに、海外にわが社の一眼カメラ製品を売り出す可能性も調査できるかもしれません。

8 B：地域的には（日本では）我が社の一眼カメラの売れ行きは非常にいいですが、まず中国市場で強固な足がかりができるまで待つべきだと思います。それから、海外で製品ラインを広げるのがいいと思います。

040

右の英語を隠し、左の日本語を見ながら、前からどんどん英語で言う練習です。

1 A: I just saw the production plans for our new digital camera model. I was surprised to see how large the advertising budget was.

2 B: Yeah, we are planning to market it mainly to Chinese consumers.
A: Really? I didn't know we were expanding into the Chinese market.

3 B: Well, we'll have to adjust prices to be able to compete, but our research shows that there is a growing market for high-end electronics in China.

4 A: Okay. But I think we'll need to gather more information about China's domestic market. Also, depending on their domestic trends, we may have to rethink what kind of functions we will offer.

5 B: That's a good idea. I'll ask our market analysis team to research what digital camera functions are most popular in the Chinese market.

6 We may have to slightly redesign some of our products to be more appealing to Chinese consumers.

7 A: We could also look into introducing our line of interchangeable-lens cameras overseas.

8 B: Our interchangeable-lens cameras have been selling very well locally, but I think we should wait until we have a solid foothold in the Chinese market. Then we can start to expand our product line abroad.

Lesson 1

041

1 左のページの日本語を見て、瞬時に英語に訳していく練習です。最初は右ページの英語を見ながら練習してかまいません。STEP 1のクイック・レスポンスと原理的には同じです。クイック・レスポンスは単語・フレーズ単位の転換練習、サイト・トランスレーションは文単位で瞬時に転換する練習です。

2 右ページの英語を手などで隠し、左の日本語だけを見て、すらすら英語が言えるようになったら、総仕上げのSTEP 4に進みましょう！

STEP 4 Reproduction 10分

イラストを見てリプロダクション

GOAL イラストだけを見て、英語ですらすらとナレーションできるようになる。

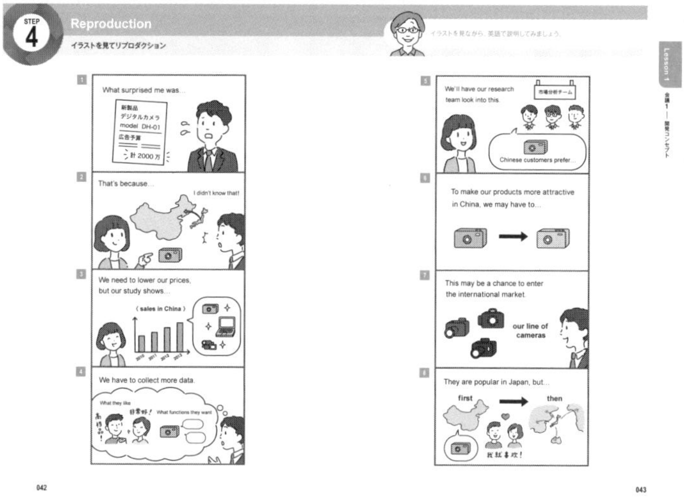

1 イラストを見て、レッスンのストーリーを英語で説明する練習です。ひとコマずつ、誰かにストーリーを聞かせてあげるつもりで、口に出して説明していきましょう。

2 うまくできない場合は、STEP 3に戻ってください。イラストのコマ番号と、STEP 3の段落番号が対応していますので、それを参考にしてください。

3 初中級者は、STEP 3までに勉強した英文を文字通り「再生」するつもりで、上級者はレッスンの英文をもとにして別の表現にトライしてみましょう。イラストだけを見て、すらすら英語で説明できるようになれば合格です！（STEP 4は難易度が高いので、だいたいできればOKです）

Lesson 1

Meeting Part 1

R&D brainstorming

会議 1

開発コンセプト

STEP 1

Quick Response

クイック・レスポンス

01

01	～の生産計画	production plans for ～
02	広告予算	advertising budget
03	市場に出す、市場	market
04	中国の消費者	Chinese consumers
05	～に進出する	expand into ～*5
06	価格を調整する	adjust prices
07	競争する	compete
08	われわれの調査によると～だ	our research shows ～
09	高級な（高額の）電子機器	high-end electronics *9
10	～についての情報を集める	gather information about ～
11	国内市場	domestic market
12	～に合わせて、～によって	depending on ～
13	再検討する、考え直す	rethink

＊5 「～に進出する」は、advance into ～、make inroads into ～、penetrate into ～ なども使える。なお「市場に参入する」なら enter the market。

＊9 high-end は "expensive and of high quality" という意味。

右の英語部分を隠し、左の日本語だけを見て、
英単語・フレーズを即座に言えるようにする練習です。

14	機能	function
15	提供する、提案する	offer
16	市場分析チーム	market analysis team
17	少し設計し直す	slightly redesign
18	～に訴える、魅力的な	be appealing to ～
19	～を調査する	look into ～*19
20	一眼カメラ、レンズ交換式カメラ	interchangeable-lens camera
21	海外に（で）	overseas
22	よく売れる	sell well
23	地域的に、地元で	locally
24	強固な足がかり（地盤）をもつ	have a solid foothold
25	製品ライン	product line *25

*19 同 examine
*25 line は “a type of product” という意味。「（同種の商品の）品ぞろえ」。

Shadowing & Repeating

シャドーイング＆リピーティング

SHA 02 REP 03

A: I just saw the production plans / for our new digital camera model.// I was surprised to see / how large the advertising budget was.//

B: Yeah, we are planning to market it / mainly to Chinese consumers.//

A: Really?// I didn't know / we were expanding into the Chinese market.//

B: Well, we'll have to adjust prices / to be able to compete, / but our research shows / that there is a growing market / for high-end electronics in China.//

A: Okay.// But I think / we'll need to gather more information / about China's domestic market.// Also, depending on their domestic trends, / we may have to rethink / what kind of functions we will offer.//

英語の音声を聞きながら口まねする練習と、
英語の音声のあとのポーズで英文を発声してみる練習です。

B: That's a good idea.// I'll ask our market analysis team to research / what digital camera functions are most popular / in the Chinese market.// We may have to slightly redesign / some of our products / to be more appealing to Chinese consumers.//

A: We could also look into introducing / our line of interchangeable-lens cameras overseas.//

B: Our interchangeable-lens cameras / have been selling very well locally,*1 / but I think we should wait / until we have a solid foothold / in the Chinese market.// Then we can start to expand / our product line abroad.//

＊1 ... have been selling very well locally ... は、現在完了進行形（have + been + *do*ing）。「ずっと～している」。（例）I have been studying Spanish for two years.（私は2年間スペイン語を勉強しています）

STEP 3

Sight Translation

サイト・トランスレーション

1 A：我が社の新製品のデジカメの生産計画を見ましたが、広告予算が大きくてビックリしましたよ。

2 B：ええ、主に中国の消費者に売り出す計画ですからね。

A：そうなんですか？　中国市場に進出するなんて、私は知りませんでしたよ。

3 B：そうですねぇ。競争できるよう価格は調整しなければならないのですが、調査によると中国では高級な電子機器（家電製品）の市場が伸びています。

4 A：わかりました。ですが、中国の国内市場に関する情報をもっと集める必要があると思いますよ。それに、中国の国内トレンドに合わせて、どんな機能をつけるか再検討しなければ…。

5 B：それはいい考えですね。市場分析チームに相談して、中国市場ではデジカメのどんな機能にいちばん人気があるのか調べてもらいましょう。

6 わが社の製品の一部を設計し直さなければならないかもしれません、中国人の消費者により魅力があるようにするために。

7 A：それに、海外にわが社の一眼カメラ製品を売り出す可能性も調査できるかもしれません。

8 B：地域的には（日本では）我が社の一眼カメラの売れ行きは非常にいいですが、まず中国市場で強固な足がかりができるまで待つべきだと思います。それから、海外で製品ラインを広げるのがいいと思います。

右の英語を隠し、左の日本語を見ながら、
前からどんどん英語で言う練習です。

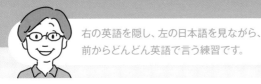

1 A: I just saw the production plans for our new digital camera model. I was surprised to see how large the advertising budget was.

2 B: Yeah, we are planning to market it mainly to Chinese consumers.

A: Really? I didn't know we were expanding into the Chinese market.

3 B: Well, we'll have to adjust prices to be able to compete, but our research shows that there is a growing market for high-end electronics in China.

4 A: Okay. But I think we'll need to gather more information about China's domestic market. Also, depending on their domestic trends, we may have to rethink what kind of functions we will offer.

5 B: That's a good idea. I'll ask our market analysis team to research what digital camera functions are most popular in the Chinese market.

6 We may have to slightly redesign some of our products to be more appealing to Chinese consumers.

7 A: We could also look into introducing our line of interchangeable-lens cameras overseas.

8 B: Our interchangeable-lens cameras have been selling very well locally, but I think we should wait until we have a solid foothold in the Chinese market. Then we can start to expand our product line abroad.

STEP 4 Reproduction

イラストを見てリプロダクション

1

2

3

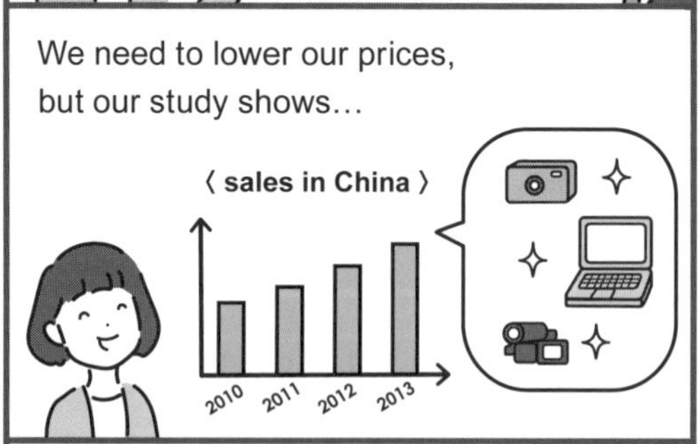

4

イラストを見ながら、英語で説明してみましょう。

5

We'll have our research team look into this.
市場分析チーム
Chinese customers prefer…

6

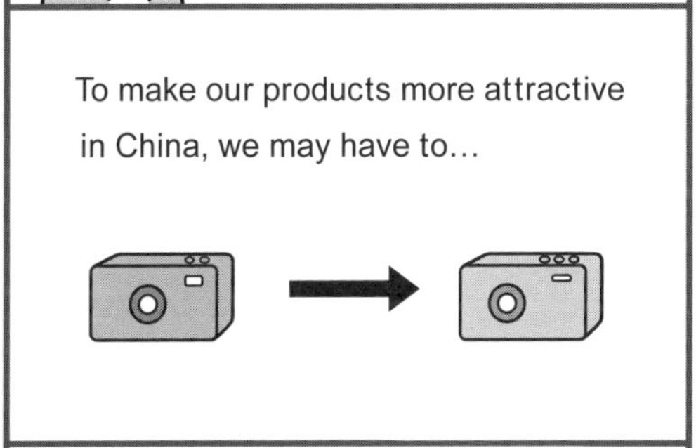
To make our products more attractive in China, we may have to…

7

This may be a chance to enter the international market.
our line of cameras

8

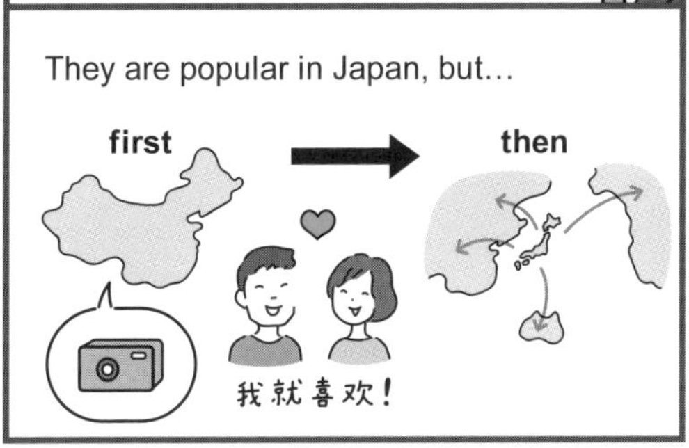
They are popular in Japan, but…
first
then
我就喜欢!

Meeting Part 2

Market segmentation

会議 2

販売層のセグメント

STEP 1

Quick Response

クイック・レスポンス

04

01
理解する、検討する　figure out *1

02
エレキギター　electric guitar

03
新規の顧客　new customer

04
新製品を紹介する　introduce a new product

05
～する準備（覚悟）をする　be prepared to *do*

06
～と異なる　(be) different from ～

07
市場の傾向　market trend

08
驚くべき　surprising

09
あなたの調査報告書　report of your research

10
～への増加する需要　growing demand for ～*10

11
～とは対照的に　as opposed to ～

12
低価格の　lower-end

13
わが社の利益を増やす　increase our profits

＊1　同 understand
＊10　demand（需要）の反対は supply（供給）。

右の英語部分を隠し、左の日本語だけを見て、
英単語・フレーズを即座に言えるようにする練習です。

14	価格の幅（帯）	price range
15	広告キャンペーン	advertising campaign
16	弊社の製品を宣伝する	endorse our product *16
17	特集する、宣伝する	feature *17
18	テレビCM	TV commercial
19	雑誌の広告	magazine advertisement
20	オンライン動画	online videos
21	若い消費者に届く	reach younger consumers
22	～の代金を払うことができる	be able to pay for ～
23	～に問い合わせる、確かめる	check with ～
24	経理部、会計部	accounting department
25	～にあとで連絡する、返事をする	get back to ～

＊16 endorse は「CMなどで、有名人が宣伝する」ことをいう。
＊17 feature は名詞では「特徴、呼び物」だが、ここでは動詞で「特定の製品を宣伝する、売り込む」。

STEP 2

Shadowing & Repeating

シャドーイング＆リピーティング

SHA 05 REP 06

A: We need to figure out / how we are going to market / our new line of electric guitars / to new customers.// Because we are introducing / a new product to a new market, / we have to be prepared / to do everything different / from how we have done it before.//

B: I have been reading / about market trends of guitar sales / in this new area, / and I have found / that flying-v style guitars are the most popular.//＊1 I think / that we should introduce this style of guitar / into our new line.//

A: That is surprising.// Could you send me / a report of your research?// I would like to see / more information about the reasons for this.//

B: Sure.// I can send it to you / by Friday.// Also, there seems to be a growing demand / for higher-end guitars / as opposed to lower-end models.// I think we can increase our profits / by increasing the quality / and also the price range of our guitars.//

＊1 flying-v style guitars は、1958 年にギブソン社が販売を始めたエレキギター。V 字を逆さにした独特なデザインで根強い人気がある。

英語の音声を聞きながら口まねする練習と、
英語の音声のあとのポーズで英文を発声してみる練習です。

A: Okay.// What kind of advertising campaign / are you planning?//

B: We are looking for popular local musicians / to endorse our products.// We would like to also feature / our products in TV commercials, / magazine advertisements and online videos.// This should help us / better reach younger consumers.// *2

A: That's a great idea, / but will our advertising budget / be able to pay for this?//

B: I'll check with the accounting department / and get back to you.//

＊2 This should help us better reach young consumers. は、help + O + *do* で「O が～するのを助ける、O が～するのに役立つ」。なお help + O + to *do* としてもよい。

STEP 3

Sight Translation

サイト・トランスレーション

1 A：わが社の新型エレキギターの新規顧客への売り込み方について、検討する（←理解する）必要があります。新しい市場に新しい製品を導入するわけですから、これまでやってきた方法とは全く違うことをする覚悟をしなければなりません。

2 B：この新規エリアにおける、ギター売上げの市場傾向について読んでいるのですが、フライング V スタイルのギターが一番人気だとわかりました。このスタイルのギターをわが社の新型ギターに導入した方がいいと思います。

3 A：驚きですね。そのリサーチの報告書、私に送ってもらえますか？ その理由について、もっと情報を見てみたいです。

4 B：もちろん。金曜日までに送ります。また、低価格のモデルよりも、高級ギターの需要が高まってきているようです。利益を増やすことができると思います、品質を高め、ギター価格の幅を広げることで。

5 A：わかりました。どういった広告キャンペーンを計画していますか？

6 B：現地の著名ミュージシャンを探しているところです、わが社の製品を（広告で）宣伝してくれるような。また、TV コマーシャル、雑誌広告、ネット動画で製品を宣伝できればと思っています。こうすることで、若い購買層に、より効率的なアプローチができるはずです。

7 A：いい考えだけど、わが社の広告予算で賄えるでしょうか？

8 B：経理部に確認して、連絡します。

右の英語を隠し、左の日本語を見ながら、
前からどんどん英語で言う練習です。

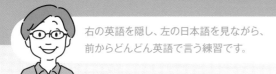

1 A: We need to figure out how we are going to market our new line of electric guitars to new customers. Because we are introducing a new product to a new market, we have to be prepared to do everything different from how we have done it before.

2 B: I have been reading about market trends of guitar sales in this new area, and I have found that flying-v style guitars are the most popular. I think that we should introduce this style of guitar into our new line.

3 A: That is surprising. Could you send me a report of your research? I would like to see more information about the reasons for this.

4 B: Sure. I can send it to you by Friday. Also, there seems to be a growing demand for higher-end guitars as opposed to lower-end models. I think we can increase our profits by increasing the quality and also the price range of our guitars.

5 A: Okay. What kind of advertising campaign are you planning?

6 B: We are looking for popular local musicians to endorse our products. We would like to also feature our products in TV commercials, magazine advertisements and online videos. This should help us better reach younger consumers.

7 A: That's a great idea, but will our advertising budget be able to pay for this?

8 B: I'll check with the accounting department and get back to you.

STEP 4 Reproduction

イラストを見てリプロダクション

1

2

3

4

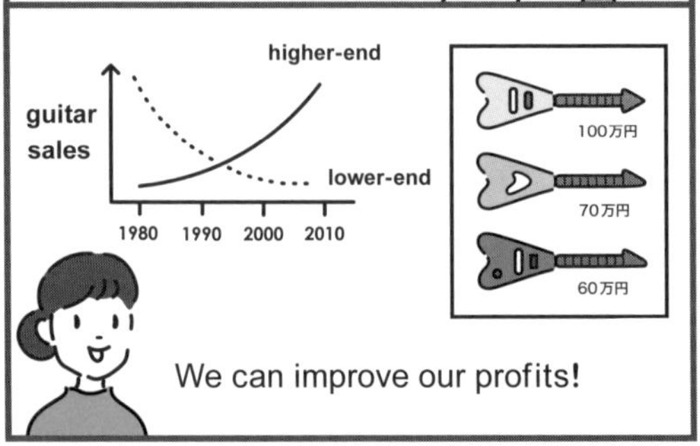

イラストを見ながら、英語で説明してみましょう。

5

6

7

8

Lesson 3

Meeting Part 3
Cost reduction plan

会議 3
コストの見直し

STEP 1 Quick Response

クイック・レスポンス

07

01

懸念する、心配する　be concerned *1

02

流通コスト、流通経費　distribution costs

03

不当に、行き過ぎて　unreasonably

04

この問題を解決する　resolve this issue *4

05

週2回の　bi-weekly

06

発送、配送　shipment *6

07

～の2倍多く　twice as much as ～

08

当初に　initially

09

コストを合理化する　streamline our costs

10

減少する　decrease

11

在庫　stock *11

12

検討する　consider

＊1 同 be worried

＊4 「問題を解決する」は solve the problem、または resolve the issue を使う。動詞と名詞の組み合わせに注意。

＊6 shipment の動詞形は ship「(商品を) 送る、配達する」。

＊11 同 inventory

右の英語部分を隠し、左の日本語だけを見て、
英単語・フレーズを即座に言えるようにする練習です。

13	恒久的な解決策	permanent solution
14	価格を上げる	raise our prices
15	「1個の価格で2個買える」の販促	"two for the price of one" sales campaign
16	コストのバランスをとる	balance the cost
17	アイデアを調査する	investigate an idea
18	～を…に基づかせる	base ~ on ...
19	量	amount
20	言い換えると	in other words
21	供給	supply
22	集中させる、焦点を当てる	focus
23	多い需要	large demand
24	売上げを伸ばす	improve our sales
25	物流部	logistics department

Shadowing & Repeating

シャドーイング＆リピーティング

SHA 08 REP 09

A: We are concerned / that our distribution costs / are getting unreasonably high.// We need to resolve this issue / before it gets worse.// Our bi-weekly shipments of our protein bars / to several chains of convenience stores / are costing almost twice as much / as we initially planned.//＊1

B: I think we can streamline our costs / by reducing our shipments / to once a week.// Also, since our sales usually decrease / in the fall season, / I think / reducing our stock at convenience stores / would be a good idea.//

A: That's a good point.// I think we should consider that idea.// But that would only be for the fall.// We need to find / other more permanent solutions.//

B: Maybe we could slightly raise our prices, / but at the same time / try a "two for the price of one" sales campaign / for a month.//

＊1 twice (three times, four times etc.) as ～ as ... は「倍数表現」で、「…の2倍（3倍、4倍 etc.)」という意味。

英語の音声を聞きながら口まねする練習と、
英語の音声のあとのポーズで英文を発声してみる練習です。

A: I see.// That could help balance /*2 the cost of our shipments.// We are investigating one more idea: / basing the amount of stock / we send to any store / on their sales percentage.// In other words, / stores that sell more / get more, / and stores that sell fewer of our bars / get a smaller supply.//

B: That could help us / focus our supply to areas /*3 where there is a larger demand.//

A: Exactly.// We hope / that this will not only adjust our shipment costs, / but also improve our sales.//

B: I'll contact the logistics department / to let them know / about our shipping schedule changes.//

＊2 That could help balance ... は、help to balance としてもよい。
＊3 This could help us focus ... は、help us to focus としてもよい。

STEP 3

Sight Translation

サイト・トランスレーション

1 A：われわれの懸念は、配送コストが非常に（←不当に）高くなっていることです。この問題を解決する必要があります、事態が悪化する前に。わが社は、いくつかのコンビニチェーンにプロテインバーを週2で配送していますが、当初予定していたほぼ2倍のコストがかかっています。

2 B：配送を週1に減らすことでコストを削減する（←合理化する）ことができると思います。また、わが社の売上げはたいてい秋には減少しますから、コンビニの在庫を減らすのは、いい考えだと思います。

3 A：いい指摘ですね。その考えは検討したほうがいいでしょう。ですが、それは秋だけに限るわけですね。一時的ではない（←もっと永続的な）他の解決策を見つける必要がありますね。

4 B：たぶん、少し価格を上げて、同時に1か月間「1個の価格で2個買える」キャンペーンをやってみてもいいかもしれませんね。

5 A：なるほど。それは、配送コストのバランスをとるのに役立つかもしれません。もうひとつ、我々が調査しているアイデアがあります。それは、店舗へ出荷する（商品の）在庫量を販売量（←売上げ比率）によって決める、というものです。言い換えると、より多く売る店舗には、より多く（の商品が）入り、わが社のバーの売上げが少ない店舗には供給量（商品の配送）が少なくなる、ということです。

6 B：そうすれば、より需要が多い地域に（商品を）集中的に出荷（←供給）するのに役立つかもしれません。

7 A：そのとおりです。これだと、配送コストを調整するだけでなく、販売量（売上げ）も伸ばせる、と期待しています。

8 B：（早速）物流部に連絡して、配送スケジュールの変更について知らせます。

右の英語を隠し、左の日本語を見ながら、
前からどんどん英語で言う練習です。

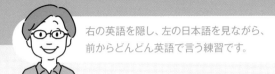

1 A: We are concerned that our distribution costs are getting unreasonably high. We need to resolve this issue before it gets worse. Our bi-weekly shipments of our protein bars to several chains of convenience stores are costing almost twice as much as we initially planned.

2 B: I think we can streamline our costs by reducing our shipments to once a week. Also, since our sales usually decrease in the fall season, I think reducing our stock at convenience stores would be a good idea.

3 A: That's a good point. I think we should consider that idea. But that would only be for the fall. We need to find other more permanent solutions.

4 B: Maybe we could slightly raise our prices, but at the same time try a "two for the price of one" sales campaign for a month.

5 A: I see. That could help balance the cost of our shipments. We are investigating one more idea: basing the amount of stock we send to any store on their sales percentage. In other words, stores that sell more get more, and stores that sell fewer of our bars get a smaller supply.

6 B: That could help us focus our supply to areas where there is a larger demand.

7 A: Exactly. We hope that this will not only adjust our shipment costs, but also improve our sales.

8 B: I'll contact the logistics department to let them know about our shipping schedule changes.

STEP 4 Reproduction

イラストを見てリプロダクション

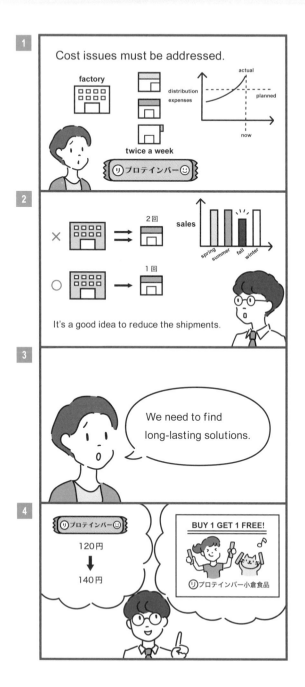

1

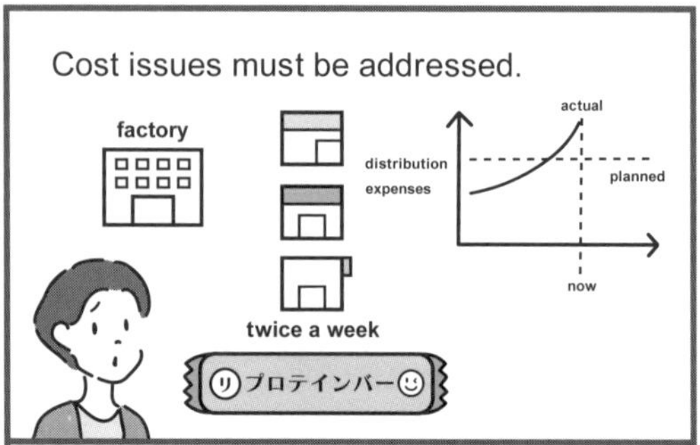

2

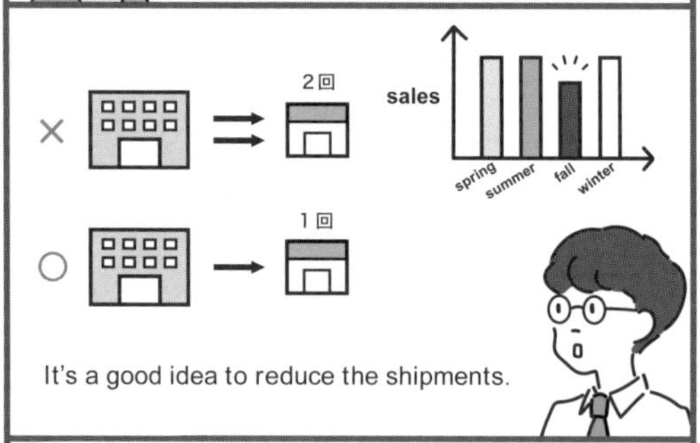

3

4

イラストを見ながら、英語で説明してみましょう。

5

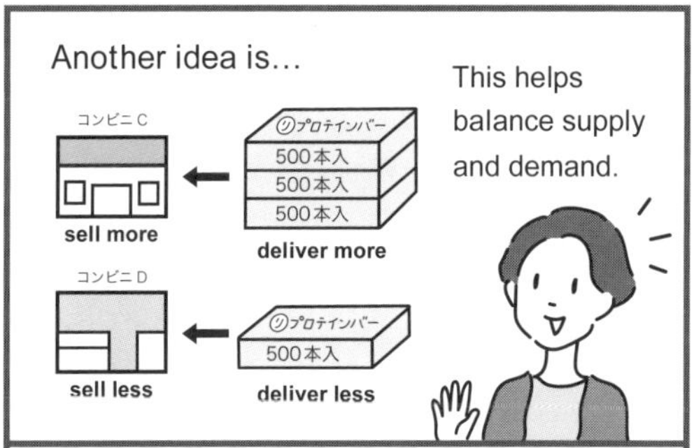

6

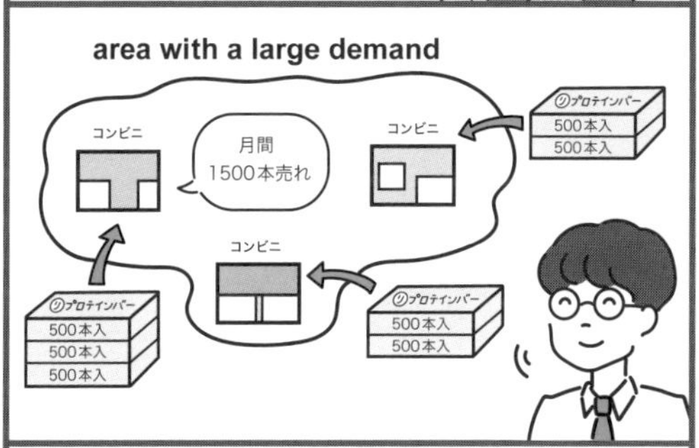

7

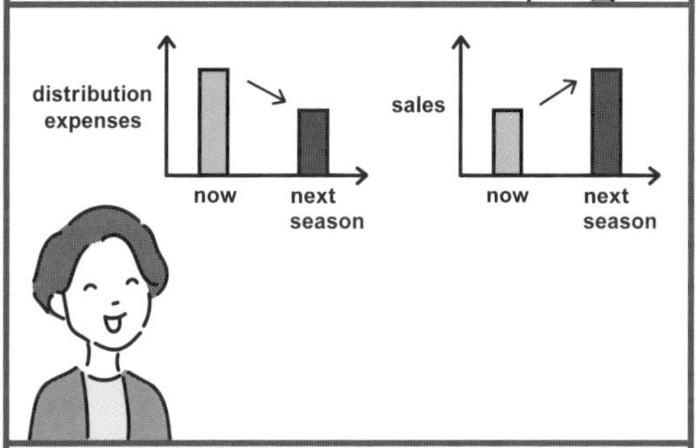

8

Lesson 4

Negotiations Part 1

Negotiating price reductions

交渉 1

値下げの提案と交渉

STEP 1

Quick Response

クイック・レスポンス

10

01	価格を下げる	lower the price
02	（価格の）見積り	estimate [*2]
03	なんとか解決策を出す	work something out [*3]
04	鉄道による輸送	shipping by train
05	～の代わりに	instead of ～
06	影響する、影響を及ぼす	affect
07	配達	delivery
08	価格設定	pricing
09	～に基づく	be based on ～
10	（燃料費等を）節約する	save on ～
11	燃料	fuel
12	～に反映される	be reflected in ～
13	～したらどうなるか	what if ～ [*13]

＊2 「見積り」は estimate、または quotation と覚える。

＊3 ニュアンスは「（苦労して）何かをひねり出す」。 同 find a solution

＊13 「～したらどうか」と提案を表す。if のあとに過去形（仮定法過去）が来ると、より丁寧な表現になる。（例）What if you bought a new car?（新車を購入したらどうですか）＊What if you buy a new car? よりも丁寧。

右の英語部分を隠し、左の日本語だけを見て、
英単語・フレーズを即座に言えるようにする練習です。

14	梱包材、荷造り用の資材	packaging materials
15	破損の危険性	risk of damage
16	～でよしとする、妥協する	settle for ～
17	見積り	quotation
18	進んで～する	be willing to *do*
19	契約を交わす、契約書に署名する	sign a contract
20	…と～を共有する	share ～ with ...
21	提案	proposal
22	上層部、経営陣	management team
23	はっきりした回答、正式な返事	definite answer
24	手に入る、入手できる	available
25	～かどうか調べる、確かめる	see if ～

Shadowing & Repeating

シャドーイング＆リピーティング SHA 11 REP 12

A: Are you sure / you can't lower the price / of your estimate?//

B: I suppose / we might be able to / work something out.// Would you consider shipping by train / instead of by air?//

A: I'm afraid / that's not an option for us.// We need those parts / as soon as possible.// Would it affect the price / if you shipped it /*1 all in one delivery / instead of two separate deliveries / like we discussed?//

B: Our pricing is based on weight, / so I'm afraid / the cost wouldn't change very much.// We might be able to save a little / on the cost of fuel, / but that wouldn't be reflected / in your order.//

A: I see.// Well, what if / we used cheaper packaging materials?//*2

＊1 Would it affect the price if you shipped it ... は、仮定法過去。「もし～したら…するだろうか？」の意味。Will it affect the price if you ship it ... としてもよいが、仮定法を使うと改まった、丁寧な表現になる。

＊2 ... what if we used cheaper packaging materials? も、やはり仮定法過去。use を使ってもよいが、used の方がより丁寧。

英語の音声を聞きながら口まねする練習と、
英語の音声のあとのポーズで英文を発声してみる練習です。

B: That would lower the price of shipping, / but it might also increase / the risk of damage to your parts.//

A: That's true.// Then I suppose / we'll have to settle for / shipping by train this time.// How much / will this affect your quotation?//

B: That would lower the cost / by about 10 percent.// Perhaps we could also lower it / another 15 percent / if you were willing to sign / a year-long contract.//

A: Alright.// I'll have to share your proposal / with our management team / before I can give you any definite answer.// If you have / a copy of that contract available, / could you send it to me later?//

B: Understood.// I'll see if / I can get a copy of the contract / to you by tomorrow.//

Sight Translation

サイト・トランスレーション

1 A：見積り金額を下げることは本当にできないんでしょうか。

2 B：弊社としてなんとか解決策を提示できるかもしれません。空輸ではなく鉄道輸送というのはお考え頂けないでしょうか？

3 A：申し訳ありませんが、それは私どもの選択肢にはありません。これらの部品はできるだけ早く必要なんです。一括配送にしたら価格に違いは出ますか、すでに話し合ったような2回の配送ではなく。

4 B：弊社の価格設定は重量に基づいています。申し訳ありませんが、価格はそれほど変わりません。燃料コストを少しは節約できるかもしれませんが、御社のご注文には反映されないでしょう。

5 A：わかりました。では、より安い梱包材を使ったらどうでしょう？

6 B：輸送費用は下がるでしょうが、部品が破損する危険性が高くなるかもしれません。

7 A：その通りですね。それでは今回は鉄道輸送で納品ということで了解しました（←我慢しなければならないでしょう）。それで見積りにどれくらい影響するでしょうか？

8 B：約10パーセント安くなると思います。さらに15パーセント下げられると思います、1年契約に応じて頂けるのであれば。

9 A：わかりました。社の上層部にその提案を伝え、それから正式な（←はっきりとした）お返事を差し上げます。契約書が一部用意できましたら、あとで送って頂けますか？

10 B：わかりました。明日までにそちらに契約書が届けられるかどうか調べてみましょう。

右の英語を隠し、左の日本語を見ながら、
前からどんどん英語で言う練習です。

1 A: Are you sure you can't lower the price of your estimate?

2 B: I suppose we might be able to work something out. Would you consider shipping by train instead of by air?

3 A: I'm afraid that's not an option for us. We need those parts as soon as possible. Would it affect the price if you shipped it all in one delivery instead of two separate deliveries like we discussed?

4 B: Our pricing is based on weight, so I'm afraid the cost wouldn't change very much. We might be able to save a little on the cost of fuel, but that wouldn't be reflected in your order.

5 A: I see. Well, what if we used cheaper packaging materials?

6 B: That would lower the price of shipping, but it might also increase the risk of damage to your parts.

7 A: That's true. Then I suppose we'll have to settle for shipping by train this time. How much will this affect your quotation?

8 B: That would lower the cost by about 10 percent. Perhaps we could also lower it another 15 percent if you were willing to sign a year-long contract.

9 A: Alright. I'll have to share your proposal with our management team before I can give you any definite answer. If you have a copy of that contract available, could you send it to me later?

10 B: Understood. I'll see if I can get a copy of the contract to you by tomorrow.

Reproduction

イラストを見てリプロダクション

1

2

3

4

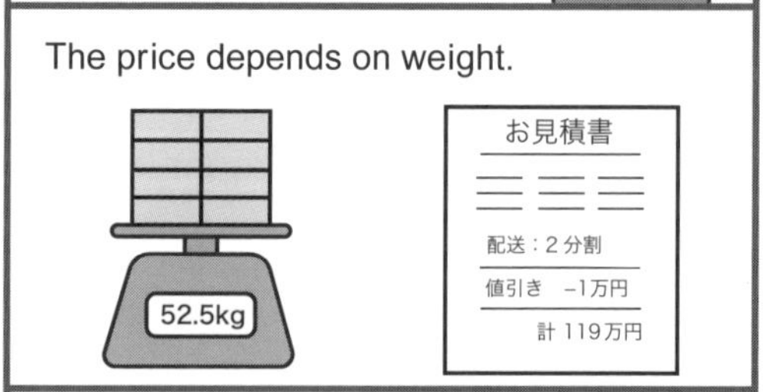

5

イラストを見ながら、英語で説明してみましょう。

6

7

8

9

10

Lesson 5

Negotiations Part 2

Price negotiations and evasion tactics

交渉 2

値下げの提案の回避

STEP 1

Quick Response

クイック・レスポンス

13

01

～で行く、～を選ぶ	go with ～

02

通常配送	standard shipping

03

速達配送	express shipping

04

価格全体	overall price

05

値引き	discount

06

大量に	in bulk *6

07

長期の	long-term

08

営業部	sales department

09

一般的に言って	generally speaking

10

～を確実にする	ensure that ～*10

11

競争力のある、～に負けない	competitive

12

産業、業界	industry

13

～を確実にする	make sure that ～

＊6 同 in large quantities
＊10 同 make sure that ～ (＝13)

右の英語部分を隠し、左の日本語だけを見て、
英単語・フレーズを即座に言えるようにする練習です。

14
（価格が）妥当な、手ごろな　reasonable

15
～を考慮すると　given ～*15

16
コストを削減する　cut costs

17
下げる、削減する　reduce

18
手配する、計画する　arrange

19
海外の関連会社　overseas associates *19

20
～と取引をする、商売をする　do business with ～

21
感謝する　appreciate

22
代わりに、交換に　in exchange

23
本当に申し訳ありません　My apologies.

24
これ以上は進めない、できない　can't go any further

25
探る、調査する　explore

＊15 同 considering ～
＊19「海外の関連会社」は overseas affiliates ともいう。なお「海外子会社」なら overseas subsidiaries。subsidiary は、通常、親会社の出資比率が 50%を超える会社をいう。

Shadowing & Repeating

シャドーイング＆リピーティング

SHA 14 REP 15

A: I don't know / if we can offer you a lower price / than what we're already offering.//

B: What if / we went with standard shipping / instead of express shipping?//＊1

A: I'm afraid / that wouldn't very much affect / the overall price.//

B: Would you be able to / give us any discounts / if we ordered in bulk / or signed a long-term contract with your company?//

A: I'll check with our sales department, / but I'm certain / that we're not offering any discounts / at this time.// Generally speaking, / we try to ensure / that our prices are competitive / with other companies in the industry, / but we also try to make sure / that they are as reasonable as possible, / given the high level of quality / that we provide.//＊2

＊1 What if we went with standard shipping ...? は仮定法過去。go を使ってもよいが、went を使うと、改まった言い方になる。

＊2 ... given the high level of quality ... この given は前置詞で、considering と言い換えられる。「～を考えると」の意味。formal な英語では頻出する。(例) Given her age, she is extremely intelligent. (年齢を考えると、彼女は非常に聡明だ)

英語の音声を聞きながら口まねする練習と、
英語の音声のあとのポーズで英文を発声してみる練習です。

B: There must be somewhere / that we can cut costs.// If reducing shipping costs and ordering in bulk / isn't an option, / then perhaps / we could arrange to introduce your company / to some of our overseas associates / who would be interested in / doing business with you.//

A: We would appreciate such an opportunity, / but I'm afraid / we can't offer any price discounts / in exchange.// My apologies, / but we really can't go any further / at this time.//

B: I understand.// In that case, / we will explore other options / and get back to you within a week.//

STEP 3 Sight Translation

サイト・トランスレーション

1 A：私どもがすでに提示している価格よりも、値下げできるかどうかわかりません。

2 B：速達配送ではなく通常配送であれば、どうでしょう？

3 A：申し訳ございませんが、それでも全体の価格にはあまり影響しないと思います。

4 B：値下げは可能でしょうか？ 大量注文するとか、もしくは御社と長期契約をしたら。

5 A：営業部に確認してみます。しかし今回は値引きはできそうにないと思っています。一般的に言って、弊社の価格は業界の他社と競争できるように努めておりますが、同時に、弊社が提供する高水準の品質を考えれば、できるだけ妥当な価格にしなければなりません。

6 B：コストカットできる部分が、どこかあるはずです。輸送コスト削減と大量注文が選択肢にないのなら、たとえば、弊社の海外の関連会社のうち何社かをご紹介することもできますが。御社との取引に興味がありそうな所です。

7 A：そういった機会は大変ありがたいのですが、残念ながら、代わりに値引きは致しかねます。申し訳ないですが、今回はこれ以上の値引きは本当に難しいです。

8 B：わかりました。そういうことであれば、他の選択肢がないか考えてみて、１週間以内にご連絡します。

右の英語を隠し、左の日本語を見ながら、
前からどんどん英語で言う練習です。

1 A: I don't know if we can offer you a lower price than what we're already offering.

2 B: What if we went with standard shipping instead of express shipping?

3 A: I'm afraid that wouldn't very much affect the overall price.

4 B: Would you be able to give us any discounts if we ordered in bulk or signed a long-term contract with your company?

5 A: I'll check with our sales department, but I'm certain that we're not offering any discounts at this time. Generally speaking, we try to ensure that our prices are competitive with other companies in the industry, but we also try to make sure that they are as reasonable as possible, given the high level of quality that we provide.

6 B: There must be somewhere that we can cut costs. If reducing shipping costs and ordering in bulk isn't an option, then perhaps we could arrange to introduce your company to some of our overseas associates who would be interested in doing business with you.

7 A: We would appreciate such an opportunity, but I'm afraid we can't offer any price discounts in exchange. My apologies, but we really can't go any further at this time.

8 B: I understand. In that case, we will explore other options and get back to you within a week.

Reproduction

イラストを見てリプロダクション

1

2

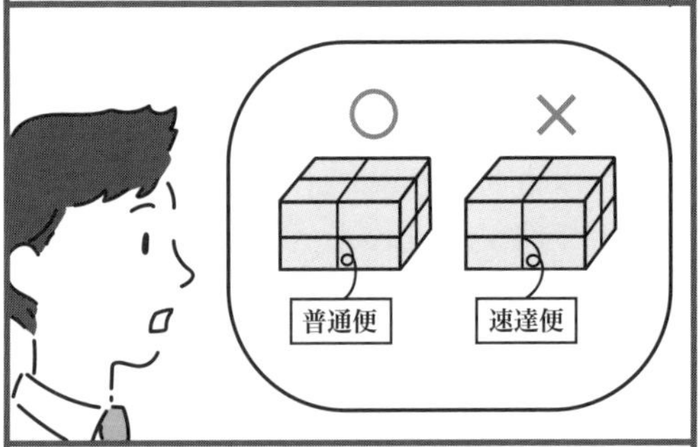

3

4

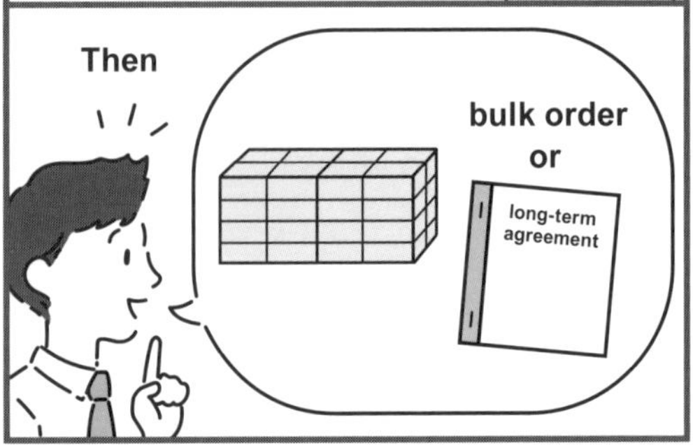

イラストを見ながら、英語で説明してみましょう。

5

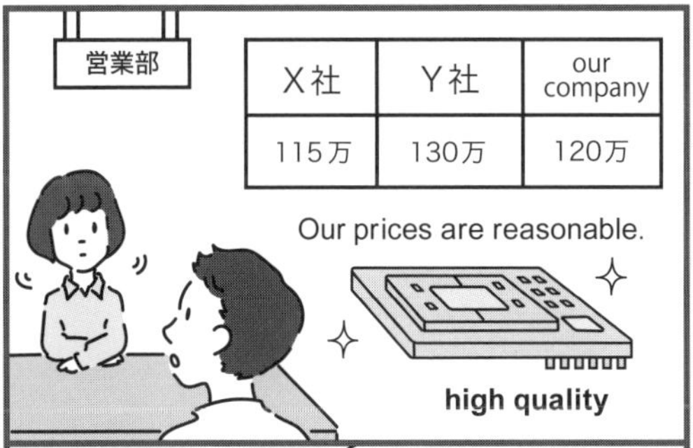

6

7

8

Lesson 5
交渉2 — 値下げの提案の回避

Lesson 6

Negotiations Part 3

Negotiating delivery date and shipping methods

交渉 3

納期と納品方法の交渉

Quick Response

クイック・レスポンス

16

01

確認する confirm

02

予定通りに on schedule

03

速達配送 express delivery

04

～が…されるよう頼む ask for ～ to be *done* *4

05

再確認する double-check

06

～も as well *6

07

施設、工場 facility

08

～である限り as long as ～

09

時間通りに、予定通りに on time *9

10

～するために in order to *do*

11

避ける avoid

12

行き違い、連絡ミス miscommunication

13

保証する、約束する guarantee

＊4 辞書には載っていないが、よく使われる表現。一般に for ～ to ... は「～が…する」と主語、述語の関係を表す。(例) I waited for the train to arrive.（私は電車が到着するのを待った）

＊6 同 too, also

＊9 on time は「時間通りに」、in time は「間に合って」。

右の英語部分を隠し、左の日本語だけを見て、
英単語・フレーズを即座に言えるようにする練習です。

14	万全の状態で	in the best possible condition
15	～に問題がある	have an issue with ～
16	検査する、調べる	inspect
17	配慮、注意	attention
18	経理部、会計部	accounting department
19	（計画などを）進める	go ahead
20	移動させる、（お金を）振り込む	transfer
21	残金、支払いの残り	rest of the payment ＊21
22	口座	account
23	財務部	financial department
24	資金、預金、お金	fund
25	機会	opportunity

＊21 「残金、残高」は balance もよく使われる。（例）The balance is due upon delivery.（残金は配達の際にお支払いください）

Shadowing & Repeating

シャドーイング＆リピーティング

SHA 17　REP 18

A: I'd like to confirm / that our shipment is on schedule / for delivery on the 11th of April.// I believed / we requested express delivery / using air mail.//

B: Well, the delivery is on schedule, / but I don't think / we received any request / for air delivery.//

A: Really?// I'll check again / with our shipping department, / but I was sure / we asked for our shipment / to be sent by air.//

B: I'll double-check our contract / as well.// In any case, / your shipment should arrive / at your facility by April 11th.//

A: I think / that as long as the shipment gets here / on time, / there should be no problem.// We asked for air shipping / in order to avoid any damage / to the shipment during delivery.//

英語の音声を聞きながら口まねする練習と、
英語の音声のあとのポーズで英文を発声してみる練習です。

B: I understand.// Sorry for any miscommunication / there may have been /[*1] between your company and ours.// I guarantee / that the shipment will reach you / in the best possible condition.// If you have any issues with the shipment / after you inspect it, / please let us know / as soon as possible.//

A: Thank you for your attention / to this matter.// I will talk to our accounting department / and tell them to go ahead / and transfer the rest of the payment / to your account.//

B: Great, / I'll let our financial department know / that the funds will be transferred.// I hope / that we will have another opportunity / to do business with your company / in the future.//

＊1 ... miscommunication (that) there may have been ...「あったかもしれない行き違い」。miscommunication (that) there was「あった行き違い」とすると、あまりに直截でぶっきらぼうなので、may + have + *done*「したかもしれない」を使って、遠まわしに表現している。

STEP 3

Sight Translation

サイト・トランスレーション

1 A：確認したいのですが、弊社が注文した品物（貨物）の納期は予定通り4月11日ですね。たしか、空輸の速達配送でお願いしたと思いますが。

2 B：ええ、納品（配達）は予定通りです。ですが、空輸というリクエストは受けなかったと思います。

3 A：本当ですか？ 配送部にもう一度確認してみますが、たしか貨物は空輸で送るようお願いしたはずですが。

4 B：私も契約書を再確認してみます。いずれにしても、貨物は4月11日までに御社の施設（工場）に到着するはずです。

5 A：貨物がこちらに予定通りに届くのであれば、問題はありません。輸送中、貨物の破損を避けるために空輸をお願いしたのです。

6 B：わかりました。御社と弊社の間に連絡不十分な点があったのであればお詫びいたします。貨物は万全の状態でお届けすることをお約束いたします。もしも点検のあと品物に問題がありましたら、できるだけ早く弊社にお知らせください。

7 A：この問題にご配慮いただき、ありがとうございます。経理部に話して、（前へ進み）御社の口座へ残額を送金するように言っておきます。

8 B：ありがとうございます。私も財務部に（御社からの）入金があることを伝えておきます。将来、また御社とお取引できる機会があればと思います。

右の英語を隠し、左の日本語を見ながら、
前からどんどん英語で言う練習です。

1 A: I'd like to confirm that our shipment is on schedule for delivery on the 11th of April. I believed we requested express delivery using air mail.

2 B: Well, the delivery is on schedule, but I don't think we received any request for air delivery.

3 A: Really? I'll check again with our shipping department, but I was sure we asked for our shipment to be sent by air.

4 B: I'll double-check our contract as well. In any case, your shipment should arrive at your facility by April 11th.

5 A: I think that as long as the shipment gets here on time, there should be no problem. We asked for air shipping in order to avoid any damage to the shipment during delivery.

6 B: I understand. Sorry for any miscommunication there may have been between your company and ours. I guarantee that the shipment will reach you in the best possible condition. If you have any issues with the shipment after you inspect it, please let us know as soon as possible.

7 A: Thank you for your attention to this matter. I will talk to our accounting department and tell them to go ahead and transfer the rest of the payment to your account.

8 B: Great, I'll let our financial department know that the funds will be transferred. I hope that we will have another opportunity to do business with your company in the future.

STEP 4

Reproduction

イラストを見てリプロダクション

イラストを見ながら、英語で説明してみましょう。

5

6

7

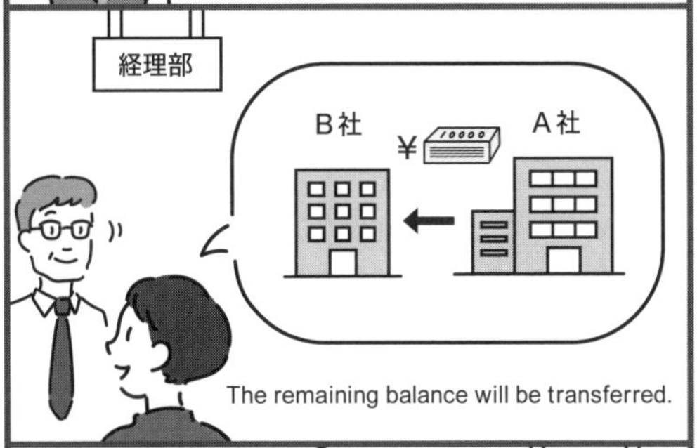

8

Presentation Part 1

Presenting air-conditioners

プレゼンテーション 1

電化製品のプレゼン

STEP 1 Quick Response

クイック・レスポンス

19

01

(商品の) 品揃え、種類　line *1

02

産業 (用) の　industrial

03

エアコン　air conditioner

04

代表する　represent

05

~にある　(be) located ~

06

職場 (環境)　workplace settings

07

目立つ、優れた　outstanding

08

顧客サービス　customer service

09

手ごろな価格　affordable prices

10

最近の出来事　recent event

11

人を~するように導く　lead someone to *do* *11

12

省エネの　energy-saving

13

効率的な　efficient

*1 lineup は「メーカーの全製品」を指すが、line は「(同種の商品の) 品ぞろえ」の意味で用いられる。
*11 lead の活用は、lead-led-led。

右の英語部分を隠し、左の日本語だけを見て、
英単語・フレーズを即座に言えるようにする練習です。

14	気温、温度	temperature
15	湿度	humidity
16	～より３分の１少ない	a third less of ～
17	結局～する	end up *doing*
18	長期的には	in the long run
19	さらに、加えて	additionally
20	大量注文、大口の注文	bulk order
21	（製品が）～台、～個	unit
22	効率	efficiency
23	できるだけ低く	as low as possible
24	お時間をいただき、ありがとうございました	Thank you for your time.
25	～から連絡がある	hear from ～

STEP 2

Shadowing & Repeating

シャドーイング＆リピーティング

SHA 20 REP 21

A: Hello, my name is Yuki Ohno, / and I would like to talk to you today / about my company's line of industrial air conditioners.// I represent ABC Air Industries, /*1 located in Tokyo, Japan.// Our company is well-known in Japan / not only for the quality of our air-conditioners / for both home and workplace settings, / but also for our outstanding customer service / and competitive, affordable prices.// As you all know, / Japan is known for / offering high quality electronics, / which we also guarantee / with our products.// Recent events in Japan / have led many companies to focus more / on energy-saving functions in their products.// Our line of industrial air conditioners / are of course efficient / at adjusting the room temperature and humidity, / but they are also able to do so / using about a third less of the amount of energy / most

＊1 formal なスピーチでは、represent「～を代表する」や on behalf of ～「～を代表して」などをよく使うので覚えておきたい。

英語の音声を聞きながら口まねする練習と、
英語の音声のあとのポーズで英文を発声してみる練習です。

air conditioners use.// This means / that you end up paying much less money / on energy in the long run.// Additionally, / we offer a 10 percent discount / on bulk orders of five or more units / at one time.// We at ABC Air Industries offer you / the high level of quality and efficiency / while keeping your energy costs / as low as possible.// Thank you for your time, / and we hope to hear from you / in the near future.//

STEP 3

Sight Translation

サイト・トランスレーション

1 A: こんにちは、大野ユキといいます。本日は弊社の業務用エアコンについてお話ししたいと思います。私は、日本の東京にある、ABC 空気工業を代表して来ました。

2 弊社は家庭用、オフィス用のエアコンの品質（の高さ）で日本国内でよく知られていますが、それだけでなく、素晴らしい顧客サービスと競争力、手ごろな価格でもよく知られています。

3 みなさんご存知の通り、日本は高性能な電化製品の販売で知られていますが、弊社の製品にもそのことを保証します。

4 最近の日本の国内事情により、多くの企業が、製品の省エネ機能をより重視するようになっています。

5 弊社の業務用エアコンは、室内温度と湿度の調整が効率的に行えるのはもちろんのこと、大半のエアコンと比べて、使用電力が約 3 分の 1 少ないのです。

6 つまり、長期的にみると電気代をかなり節約することができます。

7 さらに、弊社は一度に 5 台以上の大量注文の場合、10 パーセント割引とさせて頂いております。

8 私ども ABC 空気工業は、高品質と高性能を提供しながら、同時に電気代をできるだけ低く抑えられるのです。お時間を頂きましてありがとうございました。近いうちにご連絡を頂けることを楽しみにしています。

右の英語を隠し、左の日本語を見ながら、
前からどんどん英語で言う練習です。

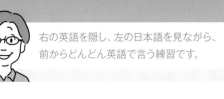

1 A: Hello, my name is Yuki Ohno, and I would like to talk to you today about my company's line of industrial air conditioners. I represent ABC Air Industries, located in Tokyo, Japan.

2 Our company is well-known in Japan not only for the quality of our air-conditioners for both home and workplace settings, but also for our outstanding customer service and competitive, affordable prices.

3 As you all know, Japan is known for offering high quality electronics, which we also guarantee with our products.

4 Recent events in Japan have led many companies to focus more on energy-saving functions in their products.

5 Our line of industrial air conditioners are of course efficient at adjusting the room temperature and humidity, but they are also able to do so using about a third less of the amount of energy most air conditioners use.

6 This means that you end up paying much less money on energy in the long run.

7 Additionally, we offer a 10 percent discount on bulk orders of five or more units at one time.

8 We at ABC Air Industries offer you the high level of quality and efficiency while keeping your energy costs as low as possible. Thank you for your time, and we hope to hear from you in the near future.

STEP 4 Reproduction

イラストを見てリプロダクション

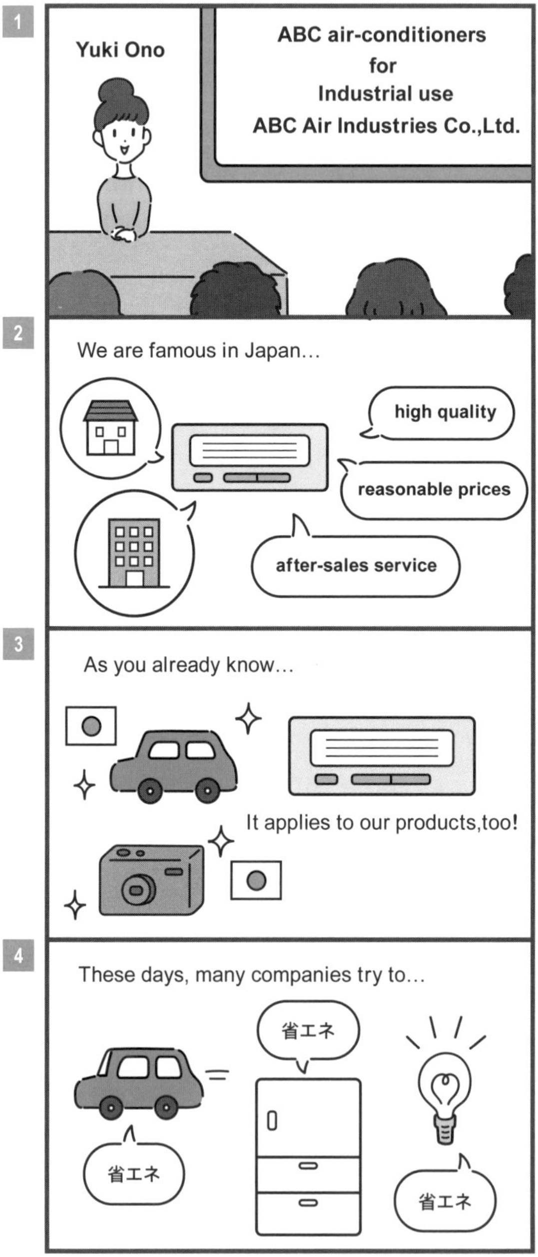

イラストを見ながら、英語で説明してみましょう。

5

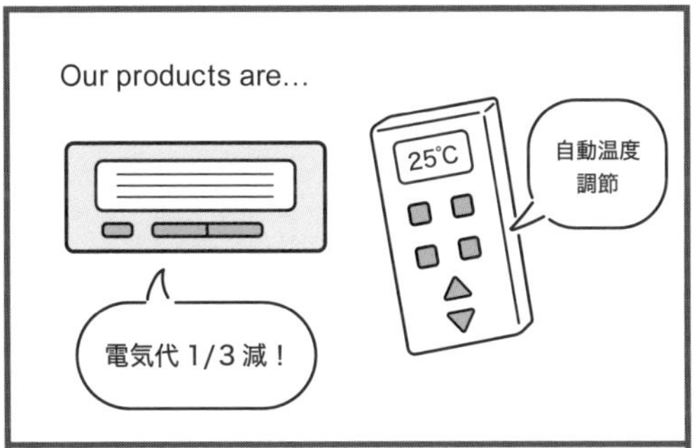

6

7

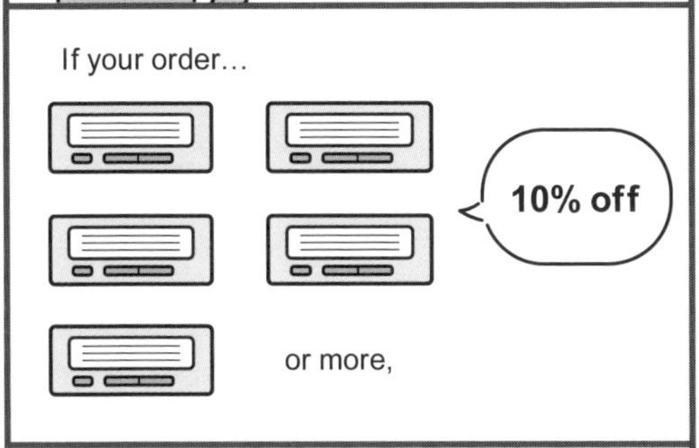

8

Lesson 8

Presentation Part 1

Question-and-answer session

プレゼンテーション 1

質疑応答編

STEP 1

Quick Response

クイック・レスポンス

22

01	保証(書)	warranty
02	海外で売られているもの(製品)	those sold overseas
03	それを聞いてうれしい	Great to hear. ＊3
04	海外への発送	overseas shipping
05	可能な時はいつでも	whenever possible
06	空輸する、空路で荷を送る	ship ～ by air
07	費用がかかる	cost
08	人が～するのを許す、可能にする	allow someone to *do*
09	顧客	client
10	心配、懸念	concern
11	取り扱う	handle
12	カスタマーサポート	customer support
13	手伝う、支援する	assist

＊3 That's great to hear. とも言う。

右の英語部分を隠し、左の日本語だけを見て、
英単語・フレーズを即座に言えるようにする練習です。

14	設置	installation
15	～に問題が発生する	have a problem with ～
16	本社	main office ＊16
17	支社	branch office
18	提供する	provide
19	技術者	technician
20	設置する	install
21	～と直接連絡をとっている	be in direct contact with ～
22	中継で送る	relay
23	大きな問題	major issue
24	交換部品	replacement parts
25	安心させる	comforting ＊25

＊16 同 headquarters, head office
＊25 同 reassuring

B: Ms. Ohno, I have a few questions / about your products.// Do you offer any warranty / on your products?//

A: Yes, we offer a one-year warranty / for all of our products, / even those sold overseas.//＊1

B: Great to hear.// And what kind of overseas shipping / do you use?//

A: Whenever possible, / we try to ship overseas by air.// This may cost a little more / than shipping by sea, / but it allows us to get / our products to our client / sooner and in better condition.//

B: I see.// I have one more concern.// How do you handle customer support?// For example, / does your company assist in the installation / of your air conditioning units?// And what should we do / if we have any problems with them?// Should we call / your main office in Japan?//

＊1 ... even those sold overseas. those は前出の複数名詞の代わりに使う。ここでは、products の代わりに用いられている。(例) The goods sold in the United States are much cheaper than those (= the goods) sold in Japan. (アメリカで売られている商品は、日本で売られている商品よりもはるかに安い)

英語の音声を聞きながら口まねする練習と、
英語の音声のあとのポーズで英文を発声してみる練習です。

A: We have several overseas branch offices / that we use to provide / the same level of customer service / as in Japan.// From these branch offices, / we are able to send technicians / to install our units / and assist with any issues you have with them / after installation.// They are also / in direct contact with our main office, / so they can relay any major issues / to us in Japan as well / and order any necessary replacement parts.//

B: That is very comforting to hear.//

A: If you have any further questions, / please e-mail me directly / and I will get back to you / as soon as possible.//

STEP 3 Sight Translation

サイト・トランスレーション

1 B：大野さん、御社の製品についていくつか質問があるのですが。製品には保証はありますか？

2 A：はい、弊社製品はすべて１年保証となっております。海外向けの製品でも（同じです）。

3 B：それは素晴らしい（←聞いて喜んでいます）。で、海外への配送方法はどうしていますか？

4 A：可能な限り、弊社では航空便で海外発送するようにしています。これは、船便よりは少し費用がかかるかもしれませんが、製品をより早く、よりよい状態でお客様のもとへ届けることができるからです。

5 B：なるほど。もうひとつ心配があります。カスタマーサポートはどのように扱っていますか？　たとえば、エアコンの設置の際に、御社のサポートはありますか？

6 また、何か問題が起こった時には、どうしたらいいでしょう？　日本の本社に電話したらいいのでしょうか？

7 A：弊社には海外支社がいくつかあり、日本と同水準のカスタマーサービスを提供するために使用しています。これらの支社から、技術者を派遣し、（エアコン）設備の設置や、設置後の問題に関してお手伝いすることができます。

8 彼らは本社とも直接連絡をとっているので、大きな問題があれば日本の私たちに問題を連絡する（←リレーする）こともできますし、必要な交換用部品を注文することもできます。

9 B：とても心強いですね（←聞いて安心させる）。

10 A：もしもさらにご質問がありましたら、私に直接メールして頂ければ、できるだけ早く回答いたします。

右の英語を隠し、左の日本語を見ながら、
前からどんどん英語で言う練習です。

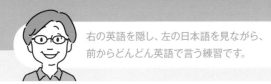

1 B: Ms. Ohno, I have a few questions about your products. Do you offer any warranty on your products?

2 A: Yes, we offer a one-year warranty for all of our products, even those sold overseas.

3 B: Great to hear. And what kind of overseas shipping do you use?

4 A: Whenever possible, we try to ship overseas by air. This may cost a little more than shipping by sea, but it allows us to get our products to our client sooner and in better condition.

5 B: I see. I have one more concern. How do you handle customer support? For example, does your company assist in the installation of your air conditioning units?

6 And what should we do if we have any problems with them? Should we call your main office in Japan?

7 A: We have several overseas branch offices that we use to provide the same level of customer service as in Japan. From these branch offices, we are able to send technicians to install our units and assist with any issues you have with them after installation.

8 They are also in direct contact with our main office, so they can relay any major issues to us in Japan as well and order any necessary replacement parts.

9 B: That is very comforting to hear.

10 A: If you have any further questions, please e-mail me directly and I will get back to you as soon as possible.

STEP 4

Reproduction

イラストを見てリプロダクション

イラストを見ながら、英語で説明してみましょう。

6

7

8

9

10

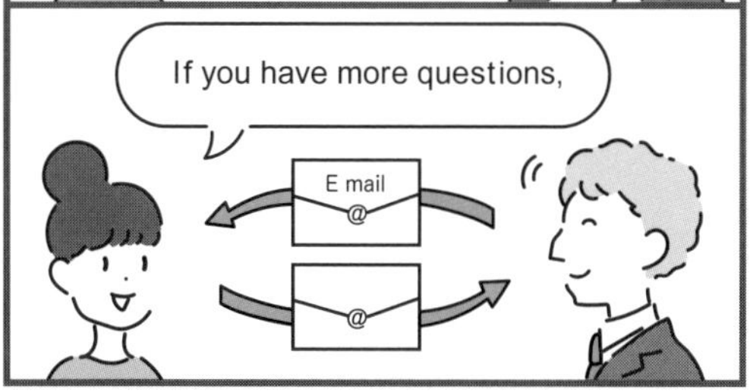

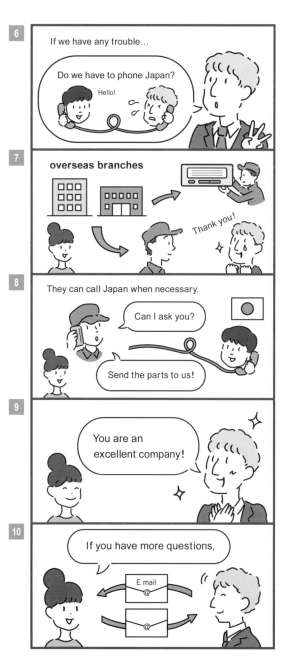

Lesson 9

Presentation Part 2
Presenting food products

プレゼンテーション 2
食品のプレゼン

STEP 1

Quick Response

クイック・レスポンス

25

01	～を代表して	on behalf of ～
02	国内で、国内向けに	domestically
03	豚骨ベースの	pork broth-based *3
04	流通	distribution
05	可能性がある	potential
06	市場調査	market research
07	増加する	increase
08	加えて、さらに	in addition
09	不景気	economic slump
10	～を求める、探し出す	seek out ～
11	選択肢	option
12	高品質の食品	quality food *12
13	おいしい	taste great

＊3　broth は肉などを煮出して作った濃いスープのこと。だし汁。
＊12　広告・宣伝の時、high quality の意味で quality が使われる。

右の英語部分を隠し、左の日本語だけを見て、
英単語・フレーズを即座に言えるようにする練習です。

No.	日本語	英語
14	～を利用する	capitalize on ～
15	現在は、今は	currently
16	人気が出る	catch on *16
17	～を…に広める	expand ～ into ...
18	発展途上の市場	developing market
19	生分解性の、微生物によって分解できる	biodegradable *19
20	環境に配慮した、環境にやさしい	eco-friendly *20
21	～するためにこの機会を利用する	use this opportunity to *do*
22	普及させる	popularize
23	広める	spread
24	自由に～する	feel free to *do*

*16 同 become popular, become fashionable
*19 「生分解性」とは、微生物の働きで無害な物質に分解される性質のこと。廃棄したあとゴミにならないので、環境にやさしい。
*20 同 environmentally friendly, environment-friendly

Shadowing & Repeating

シャドーイング＆リピーティング

SHA 26 REP 27

A: Good evening, my name is Ryo Suzuki.// On behalf of my company, Niko-niko Noodles, / I'd like to introduce / our new instant noodle product, / which we would like to make here domestically.// We would like to bring / our spicy pork broth-based instant noodle soup, / which is very popular in Japan, / to this country for distribution.// We believe / that there is a strong potential market / for this product / based on our market research.// Our research shows / that sales of spicy food / usually increase greatly in the winter season.// In addition, / the economic slump has led many people / to seek out less expensive options, / even in the food market.// We plan to offer quality food / that tastes great / for an affordable price.// We also plan to capitalize on the fact / that the quality of instant noodles / currently being offered domestically /＊1 is much lower than it is in Japan.//

＊1　instant noodles currently being offered domestically　being + *done* は「～されつつある」という意味の分詞で、前の instant noodles を修飾している。次の 2 つの違いに注意。（例）a picture painted by Taro Okamoto（岡本太郎が描いた絵）＊「完了」を表す。a picture being painted by Taro Okamoto（岡本太郎が制作中の絵）＊「進行中」を表す。

英語の音声を聞きながら口まねする練習と、
英語の音声のあとのポーズで英文を発声してみる練習です。

We feel that / if this product catches on, / it could give us a chance / to expand our line of products / into this still developing market.// Of course, just as in Japan, / we will be using / biodegradable, eco-friendly packaging / for our products here as well.// We hope to be able to use this opportunity / to help popularize eco-friendly products, / and spread new types of / affordable Japanese food products abroad.// Thank you for listening, / and please feel free / to ask me any questions.//

STEP 3

Sight Translation

サイト・トランスレーション

1 A: こんばんは、私は鈴木亮といいます。ニコニコ麺食品を代表し、即席めんの新製品をご紹介いたします。それをここで国内向けに生産したいと思っています。

2 弊社の、辛い豚骨ベースの即席めんスープは、日本では非常に人気があり、これをこちらの国に持ち込み、販売したいと思います。弊社の市場調査により、この製品の市場として強い可能性があると信じています。

3 弊社のリサーチによれば、辛い食品の売上げは、たいてい冬の季節に大きく増加します。さらに、不景気で多くの人がより安いものを求める傾向が続いていますが、食品業界も（同じです）。

4 われわれは、手ごろな価格で味のよい高品質な製品を提供することを計画しています。

5 また、事実を利用したいとも考えています、現在こちらの国内で提供されている即席めんの質は、日本のものよりずっと低いという。

6 もしもこの製品に人気が出れば、まだ発展途上のこの市場において弊社の製品を広めていくチャンスになるかもしれません。

7 もちろん、日本同様こちらでも、製品には、生分解性の、環境にやさしい包装を使用する予定です。

8 われわれはこの機会を利用して、環境にやさしい製品を広め、新しい手ごろな価格の日本食品を海外へ広めるお手伝いができればと願っています。ご清聴ありがとうございました。ご自由にご質問ください。

右の英語を隠し、左の日本語を見ながら、
前からどんどん英語で言う練習です。

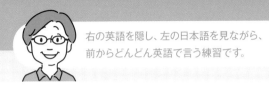

1 A: Good evening, my name is Ryo Suzuki. On behalf of my company, Niko-niko Noodles, I'd like to introduce our new instant noodle product, which we would like to make here domestically.

2 We would like to bring our spicy pork broth-based instant noodle soup, which is very popular in Japan, to this country for distribution. We believe that there is a strong potential market for this product based on our market research.

3 Our research shows that sales of spicy food usually increase greatly in the winter season. In addition, the economic slump has led many people to seek out less expensive options, even in the food market.

4 We plan to offer quality food that tastes great for an affordable price.

5 We also plan to capitalize on the fact that the quality of instant noodles currently being offered domestically is much lower than it is in Japan.

6 We feel that if this product catches on, it could give us a chance to expand our line of products into this still developing market.

7 Of course, just as in Japan, we will be using biodegradable, eco-friendly packaging for our products here as well.

8 We hope to be able to use this opportunity to help popularize eco-friendly products, and spread new types of affordable Japanese food products abroad. Thank you for listening, and please feel free to ask me any questions.

STEP 4

Reproduction

イラストを見てリプロダクション

1

2

3

4

イラストを見ながら、英語で説明してみましょう。

5

6

7

8

Lesson 10

Presentation Part 2
Question-and-answer session

プレゼンテーション 2
質疑応答編

STEP 1

Quick Response

クイック・レスポンス　28

01	～に関する、関して	concerning ～[*1]
02	合法性、適法性	legality
03	ある、特定の	certain
04	原料、(料理の) 材料	ingredient
05	認可する	approve
06	消費	consumption
07	広告	advertisement
08	～に狙いを定める	aim at ～
09	特に	specifically
10	限定的な	limited
11	今のところ	so far
12	追加の、さらなる	additional
13	戦略	strategy

＊1 回 about, regarding

右の英語部分を隠し、左の日本語だけを見て、
英単語・フレーズを即座に言えるようにする練習です。

14	～に相談する	consult with ～
15	企業、会社	firm *15
16	公開する、発売する	release
17	巧みに計画された、十分に練った	well-planned
18	競争的優位	competitive advantage *18
19	屋外の広告板	billboard
20	（新製品を）売り込む	push
21	香辛料のきいた、辛い味の	spicy-flavored
22	ごく普通の	pretty common
23	料理	cuisine *23
24	～と調子があっている、調和している	be in tune with ～
25	感性、感受性	sensibility

*15 類 company, business, enterprise, corporation
*18 同 competitive edge
*23 類 cooking

STEP 2 Shadowing & Repeating

シャドーイング＆リピーティング

SHA 29 REP 30

B: Excuse me, Mr. Suzuki, / may I ask you a few questions / about your new products?// Have you looked into any issues / concerning the legality / of certain ingredients in our country?//

A: Yes, we have made sure / that all of our ingredients / have been approved for consumption /＊1 in this country.// Our product packaging / has also been approved for sale.//

B: Okay.// My other main concern is / your PR campaign.// What kind of advertising / are you planning?// Have you prepared any advertisements / aimed specifically at / the domestic market here?//

A: To be honest, / we have prepared / a limited advertising campaign so far, / but we are also looking for / additional PR strategies / and consulting with local PR firms.// We hope to have our advertisements ready / at least one month before / we release our products.//

＊1 ... have been approved ... have + been + *done*「～されている」は現在完了（have + *done*）と受け身（be + *done*）が合体してできた形。（例）The book has been translated into 30 languages.（その本は 30 か国語に翻訳されている）

英語の音声を聞きながら口まねする練習と、
英語の音声のあとのポーズで英文を発声してみる練習です。

B: I appreciate your trying to work /*2 with local advertisement companies.// I think / a well-planned advertising strategy / can give your products / a competitive advantage in the market here.//

A: Yes, we hope so.// We hope to have our advertisements / on billboards, in magazines / and even on television.//

B: I also find it interesting / that you have decided / to push spicy-flavored products / in the winter season.// Where did that idea come from?//

A: Actually, / this is a pretty common idea in Japan.// Japanese cuisine is very much / in tune with the changes of the seasons.// We hope / that bringing these kinds of Japanese sensibilities, / we can offer something new / to the market here.//

＊2 I appreciate your trying to work ... 動名詞（*do*ing）に意味上の主語をつける場合、代名詞の所有格を用いるのが原則。（例）Would you mind my smoking here?（ここで私がたばこを吸ってもかまいませんか）

STEP 3 Sight Translation

サイト・トランスレーション

1 B：すみません、鈴木さん。新製品についていくつか質問してもいいでしょうか？我が国で使用できる食材の適法性について調査されましたか？

2 A：はい、（使用している）食材のすべてが、この国で食用に認可されたものであることを確認しています。製品パッケージも、販売認可されたものです。

3 B：わかりました。もう一つ非常に気になっているのは、御社のPRキャンペーンについてです。どのような広告を計画していますか？ 特に我が国の国内市場に狙いを定めた広告を準備していますか？

4 A：正直に申し上げて、今のところは限定的な広告キャンペーンしか準備していません。ですが、追加のPR戦略を検討しており、現地のPR会社に相談しているところです。弊社としては、少なくとも製品発売の1か月前に広告準備ができるようにしたいと考えています。

5 B：御社が現地の広告会社と協力しようとしているのは評価します（ありがたいことです）。広告戦略を十分に練れば、我が国の市場で御社の製品は競争的優位に立てるでしょう。

6 A：ええ、そう願っています。広告は野外広告、雑誌掲載、テレビにも出せればと思っています。

7 B：また興味深いのは、冬の時期に辛い味の製品を売り込もうと決断されたことです。どこからそのアイデアは来たのですか？

8 A：実は、日本では、これはごく普通の考えなんです。日本料理は、季節の変化と密接につながっています。こうした日本人の感性を持ち込み、貴国の市場に新風を吹き込めれば（←何か新しいものを提案できれば）と思っています。

右の英語を隠し、左の日本語を見ながら、
前からどんどん英語で言う練習です。

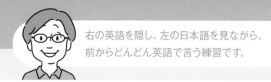

1 B: Excuse me, Mr. Suzuki, may I ask you a few questions about your new products? Have you looked into any issues concerning the legality of certain ingredients in our country?

2 A: Yes, we have made sure that all of our ingredients have been approved for consumption in this country. Our product packaging has also been approved for sale.

3 B: Okay. My other main concern is your PR campaign. What kind of advertising are you planning? Have you prepared any advertisements aimed specifically at the domestic market here?

4 A: To be honest, we have prepared a limited advertising campaign so far, but we are also looking for additional PR strategies and consulting with local PR firms. We hope to have our advertisements ready at least one month before we release our products.

5 B: I appreciate your trying to work with local advertisement companies. I think a well-planned advertising strategy can give your products a competitive advantage in the market here.

6 A: Yes, we hope so. We hope to have our advertisements on billboards, in magazines and even on television.

7 B: I also find it interesting that you have decided to push spicy-flavored products in the winter season. Where did that idea come from?

8 A: Actually, this is a pretty common idea in Japan. Japanese cuisine is very much in tune with the changes of the seasons. We hope that bringing these kinds of Japanese sensibilities, we can offer something new to the market here.

STEP 4

Reproduction

イラストを見てリプロダクション

1

2

3

4

イラストを見ながら、英語で説明してみましょう。

5

6

7

8

Lesson 11

Dealing with complaints Part 1

Making a complaint

クレーム対応 1

クレームをする

Quick Response

クイック・レスポンス

31

01	～のことで電話する	call about ～
02	ブレーキパッド	brake pad
03	～だけでなく…もまた	not only ～ (but) also ...
04	～と交換する（される）	be replaced with ～
05	すぐに	immediately
06	深刻な問題	serious problem
07	物流	logistics
08	すぐに	right away
09	正式な、公式な	formal
10	クレーム（の文書）	complaint ＊10
11	今週末までに	by the end of this week
12	どれくらい早く	how soon
13	～するよう最善を尽くす	try our best to *do*

＊10 日本語で言う「クレーム」は claim ではなく complaint という。（例）It is important to handle customer complaints properly.（顧客からのクレームは適切に処理することが大切だ）

右の英語部分を隠し、左の日本語だけを見て、
英単語・フレーズを即座に言えるようにする練習です。

14	(荷物が) 速達で【副】	express
15	全面的に	fully
16	～の費用を負担する	cover the cost for ～
17	安全な、しっかりとした	secure
18	ロット、出荷分	lot
19	破損する、傷つく	get damaged
20	謝罪する	apologize
21	不都合、迷惑	inconvenience
22	値引きする【動】	discount
23	成り行きを見る、様子を見る	wait to see *23
24	今後の注文	further orders
25	私に知らせる	let me know

*23 同 wait and see

STEP 2

Shadowing & Repeating

シャドーイング＆リピーティング

SHA 32 REP 33

A: Hi, I'm calling about the shipment / of brake pads you sent us.// Not only / was the delivery two days late, /*1 the parts were also too damaged / to use.// Since we've already signed a contract / with your company, / we expect the parts / to be replaced with new ones / and shipped to us immediately.//

B: I'm sorry to hear / you had issues with our product.//*2 This is a serious problem / and we will do everything we can / to make sure / this does not happen again.// I will tell our production and logistics departments / to arrange a new order of brake pads / to be shipped to you / right away.//

A: Okay.// We'll be sending a formal complaint / with photos of the damage / to your office by the end of this week.// How soon will you be able to / send the new shipment?//

＊1 元の文はThe delivery was two days late. だが、否定を表す語句（not only）が文頭に出たため、倒置がおこっている。

＊2 ... you had issues with our product. ここではissuesをproblemsと置き換えても通じるが、ビジネスやformalな場面ではissueが好まれる。problemよりもissueの方が、より中立的で否定的なニュアンスが含まれないため。

英語の音声を聞きながら口まねする練習と、
英語の音声のあとのポーズで英文を発声してみる練習です。

B: We will try our best / to ship the parts express by Wednesday, / so they should arrive on Friday.// We will fully cover the cost / for the replacement parts / as well as shipping.//

A: Alright.// We'll be expecting the new shipment on Friday.// Please make sure / the packaging is secure / so this lot does not get damaged.//

B: We will.// I apologize again / for the inconvenience.// Please allow us / to discount your next order / by 10 percent.//

A: We'll wait to see / the condition of the replacement parts / before we consider any further orders.//

B: I understand.// Please let me know / if you have any more questions, / comments or issues.//

STEP 3

Sight Translation

サイト・トランスレーション

1 A：こんにちは。そちらから送られてきたブレーキパッド（の貨物）のことで電話しています。納品が2日遅れただけでなく、部品は損傷が激しくて使えません。御社と契約書を交わしていますから、部品を新しいものに交換して、すぐにこちらに送って頂きたいのですが。

2 B：弊社の製品に関して問題があったとのこと、申し訳ありません。これは深刻な問題ですし、今後このようなことが二度と起こらないよう、できるだけの努力は払うつもりです。私から弊社の製造部と物流部に連絡して、ブレーキパッドの新規注文を手配し、すぐに御社に発送します。

3 A：わかりました。正式なクレーム文書をお送りします、破損した写真をつけて、そちらのオフィス宛てに、今週中に。新しい部品（←貨物）はいつ頃発送できますか？

4 B：水曜日までに部品を速達便で発送できるよう全力を尽くしますので、金曜日にはお届けできるはずです。配送とお取替えの部品の費用はすべてこちらで負担いたします。

5 A：わかりました。新しい品物が金曜日に到着するのを待っています。くれぐれも梱包は万全にして、今回の出荷分（←ロット）は破損しないようにしてください。

6 B：もちろんです。ご迷惑をお掛けしましたこと、重ねてお詫びします。次回のご注文分は10パーセント値引きさせてください。

7 A：まずは（←待って）交換部品の状態を確認してから、今後の注文について検討したいと思います。

8 B：わかりました。他にもご質問や、ご意見、問題などがありましたらお知らせください。

右の英語を隠し、左の日本語を見ながら、
前からどんどん英語で言う練習です。

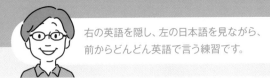

1 A: Hi, I'm calling about the shipment of brake pads you sent us. Not only was the delivery two days late, the parts were also too damaged to use. Since we've already signed a contract with your company, we expect the parts to be replaced with new ones and shipped to us immediately.

2 B: I'm sorry to hear you had issues with our product. This is a serious problem and we will do everything we can to make sure this does not happen again. I will tell our production and logistics departments to arrange a new order of brake pads to be shipped to you right away.

3 A: Okay. We'll be sending a formal complaint with photos of the damage to your office by the end of this week. How soon will you be able to send the new shipment?

4 B: We will try our best to ship the parts express by Wednesday, so they should arrive on Friday. We will fully cover the cost for the replacement parts as well as shipping.

5 A: Alright. We'll be expecting the new shipment on Friday. Please make sure the packaging is secure so this lot does not get damaged.

6 B: We will. I apologize again for the inconvenience. Please allow us to discount your next order by 10 percent.

7 A: We'll wait to see the condition of the replacement parts before we consider any further orders.

8 B: I understand. Please let me know if you have any more questions, comments or issues.

STEP 4 Reproduction

イラストを見てリプロダクション

1

2

3

4

イラストを見ながら、英語で説明してみましょう。

5

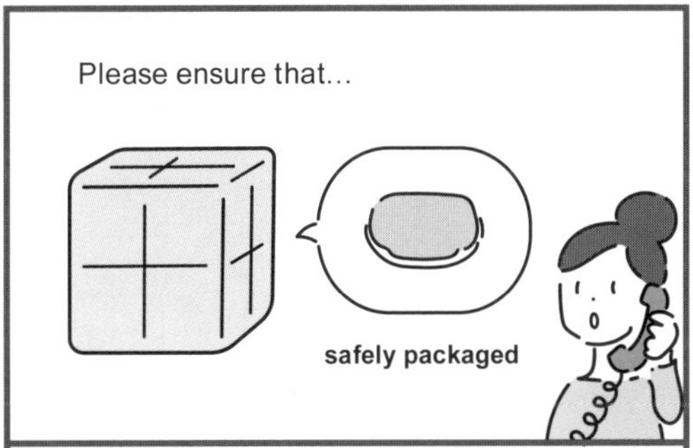

6

7

8

Lesson 12

Dealing with complaints Part 2

Receiving a complaint

クレーム対応 2

クレームを受ける

STEP 1

Quick Response

クイック・レスポンス

34

01

お知らせいただき、ありがとうございます | Thank you for letting us know.

02

〜に満足する | be satisfied with 〜

03

詳細 | detail

04

エールビール | ale beer *4

05

〜であるのに、けれども | even though 〜*5

06

（料金を）請求する | charge

07

別に、別々に | separately

08

メインの注文 | main order

09

予備の倉庫 | backup warehouse

10

主力工場 | main factory

11

追跡番号 | tracking number

12

〜を調べる | look up 〜

13

〜のようだ | it seems that 〜

＊4 日本や北米では lager beer（ラガービール）が主流。ale beer はイギリスやヨーロッパでよく飲まれる、香りやコクが強いビール。

＊5 even though は though を強調した言い方。（例）Even though I studied very hard, I did not score well.（一生懸命勉強したけれど、いい点数は取れなかった）

右の英語部分を隠し、左の日本語だけを見て、
英単語・フレーズを即座に言えるようにする練習です。

14	～に到着する	arrive at ～
15	税関で	at customs
16	～に（間に合って）到着する	make it to ～
17	時間通りに、期日通りに	on time
18	～の埋め合わせをする	make up for ～*18
19	無料で	free of charge
20	（物事を）説明する	explain things
21	その申し出を受け入れる	accept that offer
22	追加の	additional
23	直接に	directly
24	～し続ける、引き続き～する	continue to *do*
25	仕える、奉仕する	serve

＊18 同 compensate for ～

Shadowing & Repeating

シャドーイング＆リピーティング

SHA 35 REP 36

A: Thank you for letting us know / about the problems you had / with your order.// I apologize again / that you were not satisfied with your order.// Could you please tell me / the details of your problem?//

B: Yes, we ordered 20 cases / of your winter ale beer, / but we only received 18, / even though we were charged / for all 20 cases.//

A: I see.// It seems / that the last two cases were shipped separately / from the main order.// We had to ship them / from our backup warehouse / instead of our main factory.// The shipment may just be delayed.// May I have / your shipment tracking number?//

B: Sure.// It's 8155 / -4818 / -6286.//

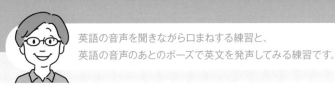

英語の音声を聞きながら口まねする練習と、
英語の音声のあとのポーズで英文を発声してみる練習です。

A: Thank you.// I just looked up your order, / and it seems / that it should arrive at your company / in two days.// It is being delayed / at customs.//[*1] I apologize / that our shipment didn’t make it to you / on time.// To make up for this, / we would like to ship to you / two cases of any one of our products / free of charge.//

B: Really?// Thank you for explaining things.// I think / we can accept that offer.// Would it be okay to send an order / for those two additional cases / by e-mail?//

A: Yes, please send it directly to me / at ellen@nobgoblinbeer.com.// I hope that we can continue / to serve you and your clients / in the future.//

＊1 It is being delayed at customs. be + being + *done*「～されつつある」は進行形（be + *doing*）と受け身（be + *done*）が合体してできた形。（例）The contract is being negotiated.（契約は交渉中だ）

STEP 3 Sight Translation

サイト・トランスレーション

1 A：今回のご注文に関する問題についてお知らせ頂き、ありがとうございます。ご注文に満足頂けなかったことを再びお詫びいたします。問題の詳細についてお聞かせ頂けますか？

2 B：えぇ、冬季限定エールビールを20ケース注文したのですが、こちらには18ケースしか届かず、それなのに20ケース分全部の料金が請求されているんです。

3 A：わかりました。どうも残りの2ケースは18ケースの注文（←メインの注文）とは別に発送されたようです。弊社の主力工場からではなく予備の倉庫から出荷しなければならなかったのです。おそらく配送が遅れているだけだと思います。お荷物の追跡番号を教えて頂けますか？

4 B：はい。8155-4818-6286です。

5 A：ありがとうございます。いま御社のご注文を調べましたが、おそらく2日後に御社に届くはずです。税関で遅れているようです。

6 荷物が期日に間に合わなかったこと、申し訳ありません。埋め合わせとして、弊社製品のどれでも（お好きなもの）2ケースを無料で発送したいと思います。

7 B：本当ですか？ ご説明ありがとうございます。その提案はお受けしたいと思います。その追加2ケース分の注文はEメールで送ってもいいですか？

8 A：はい、私に直接送ってください。ellen@nobgoblinbeer.comです。弊社としては、引き続き御社および御社のクライアントとお取引できればと思っています。

右の英語を隠し、左の日本語を見ながら、
前からどんどん英語で言う練習です。

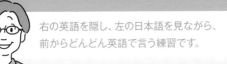

1 A: Thank you for letting us know about the problems you had with your order. I apologize again that you were not satisfied with your order. Could you please tell me the details of your problem?

2 B: Yes, we ordered 20 cases of your winter ale beer, but we only received 18, even though we were charged for all 20 cases.

3 A: I see. It seems that the last two cases were shipped separately from the main order. We had to ship them from our backup warehouse instead of our main factory. The shipment may just be delayed. May I have your shipment tracking number?

4 B: Sure. It's 8155-4818-6286.

5 A: Thank you. I just looked up your order, and it seems that it should arrive at your company in two days. It is being delayed at customs.

6 I apologize that our shipment didn't make it to you on time. To make up for this, we would like to ship to you two cases of any one of our products free of charge.

7 B: Really? Thank you for explaining things. I think we can accept that offer. Would it be okay to send an order for those two additional cases by e-mail?

8 A: Yes, please send it directly to me at ellen@nobgoblinbeer.com. I hope that we can continue to serve you and your clients in the future.

STEP 4 Reproduction

イラストを見てリプロダクション

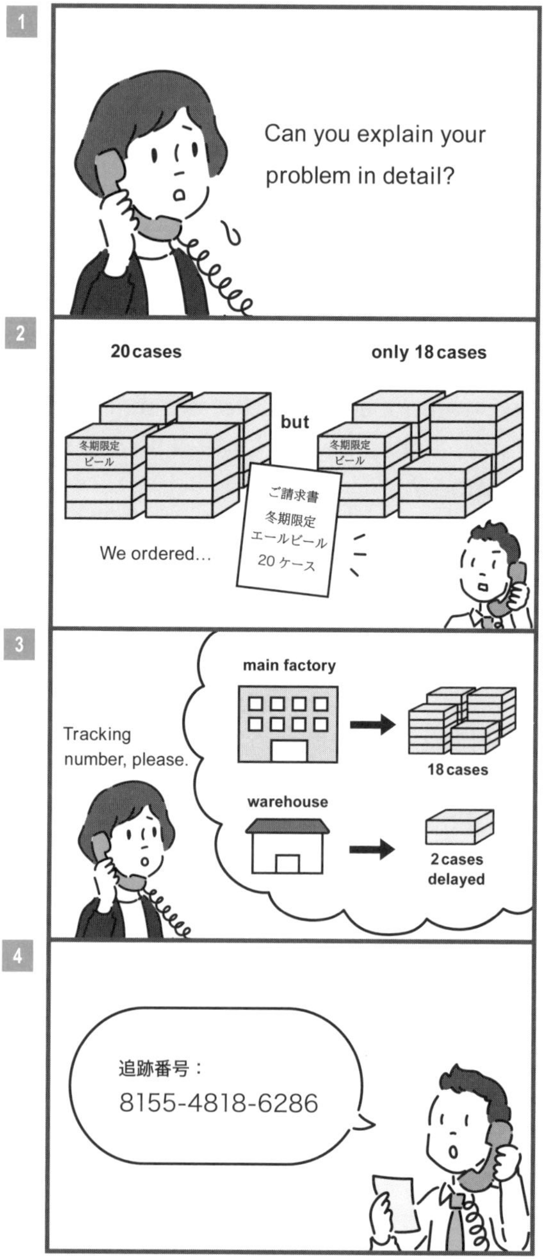

イラストを見ながら、英語で説明してみましょう。

5

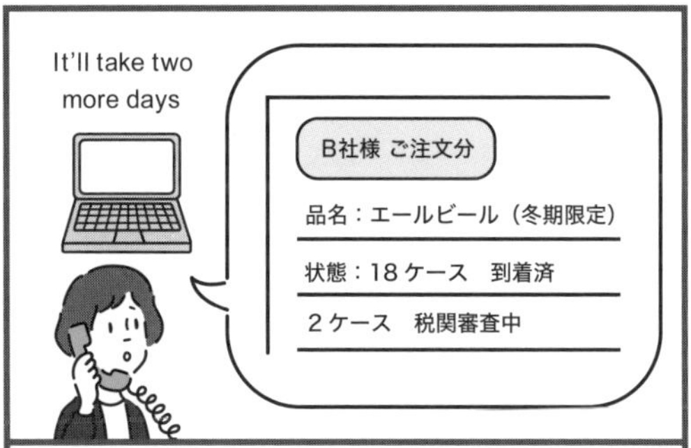

6

7

8

Lesson 13

Asking your junior to do something for you

部下への仕事の依頼

STEP 1

Quick Response

クイック・レスポンス

37

01	（人）に頼みごとをする	ask someone a favor
02	時間がある	have got some time *2
03	何をお手伝いしましょう?	What can I do for you?
04	提案	proposal
05	プレゼンする【動】	present
06	～に取り組む	work on ～
07	それがどうしたのか	What about it?
08	病欠の電話をする	call in sick
09	唯一の～	the only ～
10	部署、部門	department
11	導入部	introduction
12	アウトライン、概要	overview

＊2 have got は have と同じ意味で用いられるくだけた表現。（例）Have you got what it takes to start your own business?（起業に必要なものは、持っていますか）

右の英語部分を隠し、左の日本語だけを見て、
英単語・フレーズを即座に言えるようにする練習です。

13	（人）が…するのに～の時間がかかる	it takes someone ～ to *do*
14	データ、資料	material
15	プレゼン	presentation
16	集める	gather
17	～に関するデータ	data on ～
18	試作品	prototype
19	含む	include
20	～の一部として	as part of ～
21	念のため、～であると確認するために	just to be sure
22	（目標について）考えが一致している	be on the same page
23	（人）に電話する	give someone a call
24	準備する	have things ready

Shadowing & Repeating

シャドーイング＆リピーティング SHA 38 REP 39

A: Hey, are you busy?// I need to ask you a favor.//

B: All right.// I've got some time.// What can I do for you?//

A: Well, remember the proposal / we were going to present at D Company / that Yukiko was working on?//

B: Yeah, what about it?//＊1

A: She called in sick today, / so I need you to finish it / by tomorrow afternoon.// You're the only other person in the department /＊2 that knows how to write a proposal / and we need to have something to present / when we visit D Company's factory / this week.// I think she's already written / the introduction and overview of the proposal, / so it shouldn't take you too long / to finish.//

＊1 ... what about it? は、相手の発言に対して「それがどうしたの？」と聞く言い方。Why do you ask? と言い換えられる。

＊2 ... the only other person ... the other + 単数名詞は「(2 つのうちで) もう一方の～」という意味。(例) the other side of the street（通りの向こう側）

英語の音声を聞きながら口まねする練習と、
英語の音声のあとのポーズで英文を発声してみる練習です。

B: Okay.// Can you send me / what Yukiko has done so far / and any other materials / you have for the presentation?//

A: Sure.// I'll email it to you now.// I also need you / to gather all the data on the new prototype / and include that in the presentation.// I'd like to present our new prototype / as part of our proposal.//

B: Okay.// Just to be sure / we're on the same page, / I'll give Yukiko a call / and ask her about the details of the proposal.// I'll be sure to have things ready / before our visit to D Company.//

STEP 3

Sight Translation

サイト・トランスレーション

1 A：忙しいかな？ お願いしたいことがあるんだけど。
B：いいですよ。時間はあります。何をお手伝いしましょう？

2 A：えっと、D 社でプレゼンすることになっていた提案、覚えてるかな。ユキコが進めていた。
B：ええ、それがどうしたんでしょう？

3 A：彼女から今日、病欠の電話があったんだ。だからこれを明日の午後までに仕上げてほしいんだ。

4 この部署で提案書の書き方を知っているのは（ユキコの）他には君だけだし、今週 D 社の工場を訪問するときに、何かプレゼンする（←プレゼンする何かを持っている）必要がある。

5 ユキコはもう提案書の導入部とアウトラインは書いていると思うから、仕上げるのにそれほど時間はかからないはずだ。

6 B：わかりました。今までユキコがやった分を送ってもらえますか。それにプレゼンのために（あなたが）持っているその他の資料も。

7 A：もちろん。いまメールで送るよ。それに新しい試作品に関するデータをすべて集めて、プレゼンに入れてほしいんだ。新しい試作品を当社提案の一部としてプレゼンしたいんだ。

8 B：わかりました。お互いの認識をすり合わせるために（←私たちが同じ考えであることを確実にするために）、ユキコに電話して提案の詳細について聞いてみます。必ず D 社訪問前に準備を整えます。

右の英語を隠し、左の日本語を見ながら、
前からどんどん英語で言う練習です。

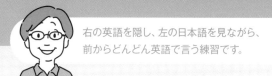

1 A: Hey, are you busy? I need to ask you a favor.
B: All right. I've got some time. What can I do for you?

2 A: Well, remember the proposal we were going to present at D Company that Yukiko was working on?
B: Yeah, what about it?

3 A: She called in sick today, so I need you to finish it by tomorrow afternoon.

4 You're the only other person in the department that knows how to write a proposal and we need to have something to present when we visit D Company's factory this week.

5 I think she's already written the introduction and overview of the proposal, so it shouldn't take you too long to finish.

6 B: Okay. Can you send me what Yukiko has done so far and any other materials you have for the presentation?

7 A: Sure. I'll email it to you now. I also need you to gather all the data on the new prototype and include that in the presentation. I'd like to present our new prototype as part of our proposal.

8 B: Okay. Just to be sure we're on the same page, I'll give Yukiko a call and ask her about the details of the proposal. I'll be sure to have things ready before our visit to D Company.

STEP 4

Reproduction

イラストを見てリプロダクション

イラストを見ながら、英語で説明してみましょう。

5

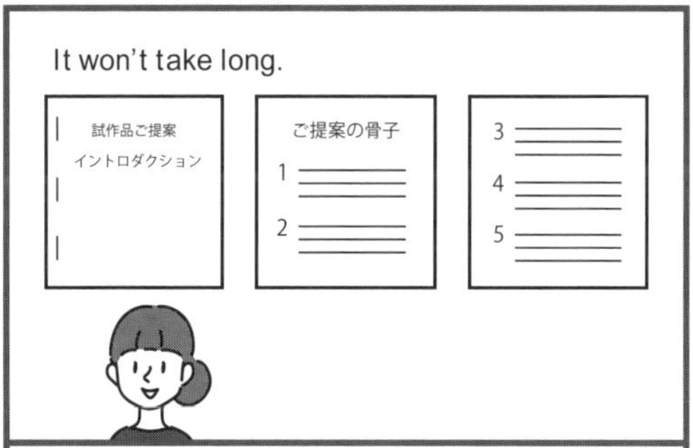

6

7

8

Lesson 14

Checking and confirming a contract

契約書の確認

STEP 1

Quick Response

クイック・レスポンス

40

01	～について話し合う	discuss
02	契約（書）	contract
03	契約書の草案	draft agreement
04	（契約の）条件	terms
05	独占権	exclusive rights
06	子供用商品	children's goods
07	～と長期契約を締結する	have a long-standing contract with ～
08	衣類	apparel
09	弊社のキャラクターイメージを使った	with our character's image
10	見落とす	overlook
11	（契約の）効力発生日	effective date
12	～について合意する	agree on ～
13	以前に	previously

右の英語部分を隠し、左の日本語だけを見て、
英単語・フレーズを即座に言えるようにする練習です。

No.	日本語	English
14	実際の	actual
15	修正する	revise
16	秘密保持契約	non-disclosure agreement *16
17	期間（時間）の制限	time restriction
18	述べる	state
19	～を…に制限する	limit ～ to ...
20	取り決め、合意	arrangement
21	（可能性が）開かれている、受け入れる準備がある	be open to ～
22	見直し、検討	review
23	延長	extension
24	～を考慮に入れる	take ～ into consideration *24
25	書き直す	redraft *25

＊16 「守秘義務契約」は confidentiality agreement ともいう。業務上知りえた秘密・重要事項を第三者に知らせない契約。cf. privileged information「部外秘の情報、公にしてはならない情報」
＊24 同 take ～ into account
＊25 類 revise, rewrite

A: There are some things / I'd like to discuss about our contract.// Our office had some questions / about the draft agreement.//

B: Yes, please continue.// I'll answer whatever I can, / and look into any questions / I can't answer at this time.//

A: The contract's terms say / that you have the exclusive rights / to use the image of our character / for your line of children's goods.// However, as you know, / we already have a long-standing contract / with another company / to sell apparel with our character's image.//

B: Ah yes, we seemed to have overlooked that.//＊1 Please let us know / if there are any other issues / with the rest of the contract.//

＊1 ... we seemed to have overlooked that. seem to have *done* で「～したらしい、したようだ」。(例) He seems to have been sick in bed. = It seems that he was sick in bed. (彼は病気で寝ていたらしい)

英語の音声を聞きながら口まねする練習と、
英語の音声のあとのポーズで英文を発声してみる練習です。

A: Right, / well, it seems the effective date of the contract / that we agreed on previously / is different from what you wrote / in the actual contract.// Please revise this.// Also, I don't see anything here / about our non-disclosure agreement.// Moreover, it seems / that there isn't any time restriction / stated in the contract.// We would prefer to limit our arrangement / to a five-year period.// After that, / we would be open to / a review of the contract / and a possible extension.//

B: Understood.// We will take these things into consideration / and redraft the agreement / and send it to you as soon as possible.//

STEP 3 Sight Translation

サイト・トランスレーション

1 A：契約書に関して、話し合いたいことがいくつかあります。弊社から、契約書草案についていくつか質問が出ました。

2 B：はい、続けてください。できるかぎりお答えします。今答えられない質問はお調べします。

3 A：契約条件にはこう書かれています。御社が、弊社のキャラクターイメージを使用する独占権を有する、御社の子供向け製品に対して。

4 しかし、ご存知のように、弊社はすでに他社と長期契約を締結しています、弊社のキャラクターイメージを使った衣類を販売するという。

5 B：そうでした。うっかり失念していたようです。契約書の他の部分にも問題があればおっしゃってください。

6 A：そうですね、どうも以前に合意した契約の効力発生日が実際の契約書に書かれている日付（←もの）と違うようです。どうか修正して下さい。それに、秘密保持に関する条文（←合意）が見当たらないですね。

7 また、契約書に期間の制限が書かれていません。弊社は5年契約に制限したいです。その後は、契約書の見直しとその後の延長を考えたいと思います。

8 B：わかりました。それらを考慮に入れて契約書の草案を書き直し、できるだけ早くそちらに送ります。

右の英語を隠し、左の日本語を見ながら、
前からどんどん英語で言う練習です。

1 A: There are some things I'd like to discuss about our contract. Our office had some questions about the draft agreement.

2 B: Yes, please continue. I'll answer whatever I can, and look into any questions I can't answer at this time.

3 A: The contract's terms say that you have the exclusive rights to use the image of our character for your line of children's goods.

4 However, as you know, we already have a long-standing contract with another company to sell apparel with our character's image.

5 B: Ah yes, we seemed to have overlooked that. Please let us know if there are any other issues with the rest of the contract.

6 A: Right, well, it seems the effective date of the contract that we agreed on previously is different from what you wrote in the actual contract. Please revise this. Also, I don't see anything here about our non-disclosure agreement.

7 Moreover, it seems that there isn't any time restriction stated in the contract. We would prefer to limit our arrangement to a five-year period. After that, we would be open to a review of the contract and a possible extension.

8 B: Understood. We will take these things into consideration and redraft the agreement and send it to you as soon as possible.

STEP 4

Reproduction

イラストを見てリプロダクション

イラストを見ながら、英語で説明してみましょう。

5

6

7

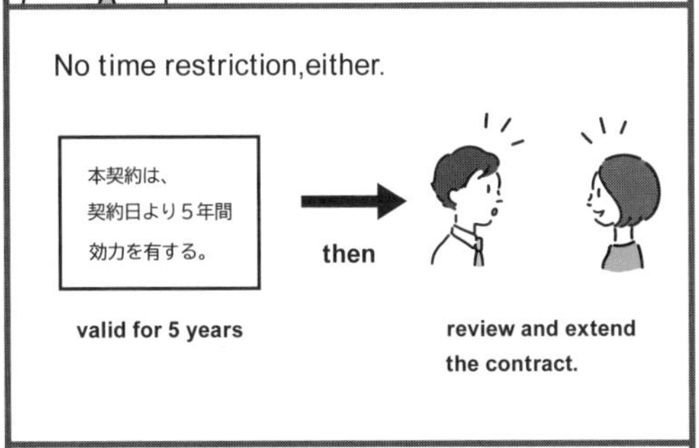

8

Lesson 15

Appealing to your boss during employee performance evaluations

人事考課でのアピール

STEP 1 Quick Response

クイック・レスポンス 43

01	人事考課、業績評価	performance review
02	～について（少し）話す	mention
03	プロジェクト責任者	project leader
04	事務費	office expenditure
05	削減	reduction
06	～を…に費やす	spend ～ on ...
07	事務用品	office supplies
08	策定する、計画する	draft
09	人時、工数	man-hour＊9
10	工場（フロア）スタッフ	factory floor staff
11	（休まずに）～を続ける	continue with ～
12	合理化する、能率的にする	streamline
13	事務費	office expenses

＊9　人時・マンアワーとは、一人一時間当たりの仕事量のこと。

右の英語部分を隠し、左の日本語だけを見て、
英単語・フレーズを即座に言えるようにする練習です。

14	労働力、従業員	workforce
15	機械オペレータ	machine operator
16	給与	salary
17	できるだけ効率的に	as efficiently as possible
18	～の可能性がある	there is a chance that ～
19	現地スタッフを訓練する	train the local staff
20	もし～の場合に（備えて）	just in case ～*20
21	ビジネス慣行	business practice
22	～に順応する、適応する	adapt to ～
23	環境	environment
24	評価	evaluation
25	聞いて頂き、ありがとうございます	Thank you for listening.

＊20 本文では、just in case は接続詞として用いられているが、副詞句としてもよく使われる。
（例）You really should take an umbrella with you, just in case.（念のため傘を持って行った方がいいよ）

For my performance review, / I would just like to mention a few things.// As I'm sure you know, / I was one of the project leaders / on last year's office expenditure reduction action plan / that helped to reduce / how much we spend / on office supplies by 37 percent.// I am also currently drafting / a new man-hour reduction plan /*1 for our factory floor staff.// My plan is / to continue with the streamlining / of our office expenses / and expand our new efficiency / to our workforce.// I hope to be able to reduce / the number of machine operators needed daily / from ten to seven people.// This will allow us / to save money on worker salaries / and make sure / that each operator is working / as efficiently as possible.// Also, I heard that there is a chance / that our company might be sending some of our staff / to our branch office in China / to help

＊1 man-hour 工数（人時）＝人×時間で、製造業でよく使われる概念。（例）The construction of each single home requires approximately 3,000 man-hours.（家を一軒建てるのに、約3,000人時必要だ）

英語の音声を聞きながら口まねする練習と、
英語の音声のあとのポーズで英文を発声してみる練習です。

train the local staff there.// Just in case I am chosen, / I have been studying Chinese / as well as international business practices.// I think / that these would give me an advantage / in adapting to the new environment quicker.// I hope that you consider these points / in my evaluation.// Thank you for listening.//

STEP 3 Sight Translation

サイト・トランスレーション

1 私の人事考課（←業績評価）のために、少しお話ししたいと思います。ご存知のように、昨年の「事務費削減アクションプラン」で私はプロジェクトリーダーの一人でした。このプランで、当社の事務用品費を37パーセント削減することに成功しました。

2 また、現在、当社工場フロアスタッフに対する工数削減の新計画草案も策定中です。

3 私の計画としては、これからも事務経費の合理化を継続し、この新しい効率化を作業スタッフ（←労働力）にも広げていきたいです。

4 1日に必要な機械オペレータの人数を10人から7人に減らすことができればと考えています。

5 これにより、人件費（←作業員の給与の費用）を削減できますし、確実に各オペレータが最大限効率的に働くことになります。

6 また、聞くところによると、一部の社員が中国支社へ配属される可能性があるとのこと、現地スタッフ訓練を手伝うために。

7 もし仮に私が選ばれたときのために、私は中国語も国際ビジネス慣行についても勉強してきました。

8 そのおかげで、私が新しい環境により早く順応できる（←順応するのに有利になる）と思っています。私の評価に、これらの事項を考慮して頂けると幸いです。聞いて頂いてありがとうございました。

右の英語を隠し、左の日本語を見ながら、
前からどんどん英語で言う練習です。

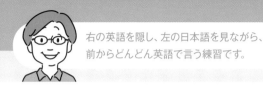

1 For my performance review, I would just like to mention a few things. As I'm sure you know, I was one of the project leaders on last year's office expenditure reduction action plan that helped to reduce how much we spend on office supplies by 37 percent.

2 I am also currently drafting a new man-hour reduction plan for our factory floor staff.

3 My plan is to continue with the streamlining of our office expenses and expand our new efficiency to our workforce.

4 I hope to be able to reduce the number of machine operators needed daily from ten to seven people.

5 This will allow us to save money on worker salaries and make sure that each operator is working as efficiently as possible.

6 Also, I heard that there is a chance that our company might be sending some of our staff to our branch office in China to help train the local staff there.

7 Just in case I am chosen, I have been studying Chinese as well as international business practices.

8 I think that these would give me an advantage in adapting to the new environment quicker. I hope that you consider these points in my evaluation. Thank you for listening.

Reproduction

イラストを見てリプロダクション

1

2

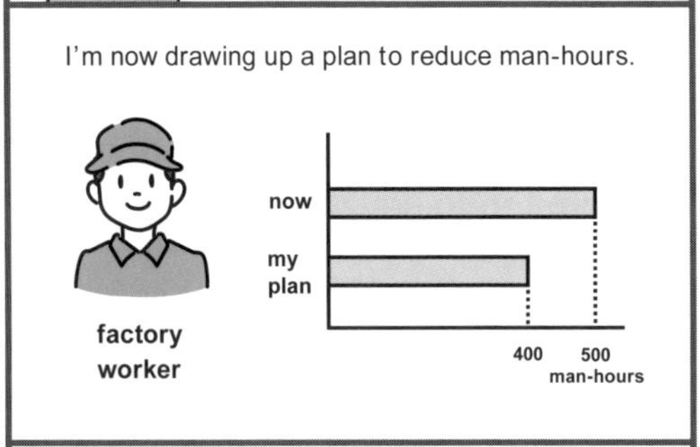

3

4

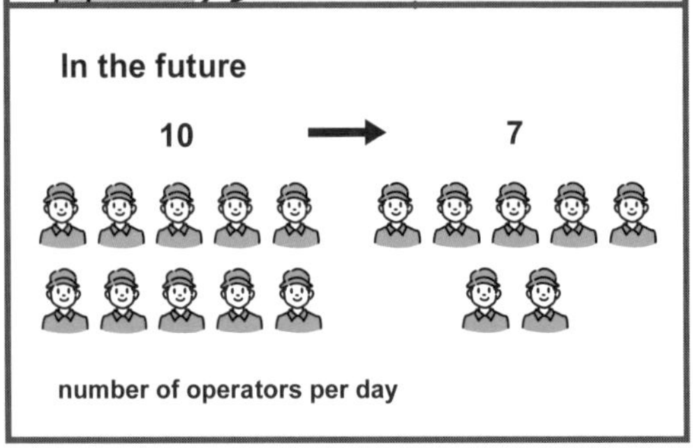

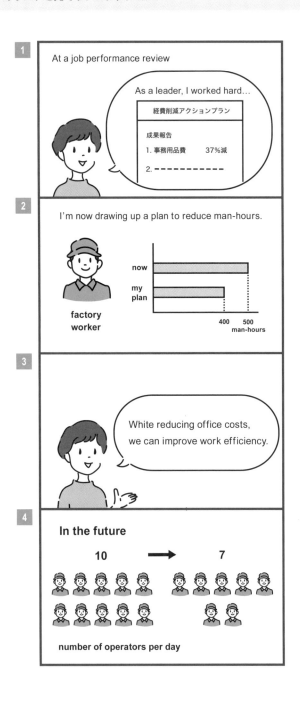

イラストを見ながら、英語で説明してみましょう。

5

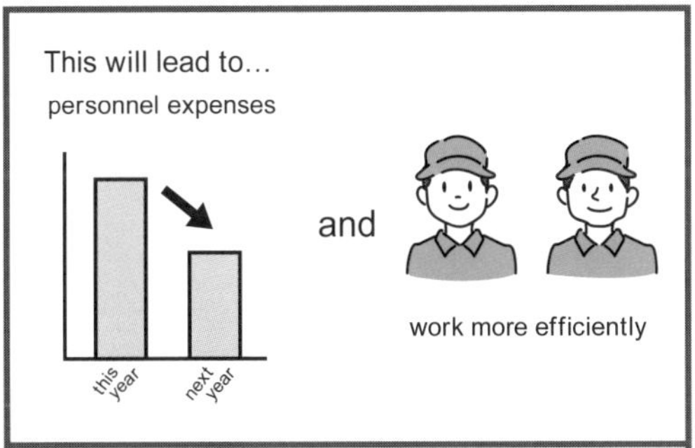

6

7

8

Lesson 16

Company introduction Part 1

Talking about your company's history and what it does

会社紹介 1

業務内容と社歴の紹介

STEP 1

Quick Response

クイック・レスポンス

46

01	出席する	attend
02	主に	mainly
03	製造する	manufacture
04	自動車部品	automobile parts
05	ウォーターポンプ	water pump
06	業務用の、工業用の	for industrial use
07	本社	headquarters
08	設立する	establish
09	創立する、創業する	found *9
10	元（前）社長	former president
11	自動車関連の	car-related
12	現実となる、実現する	become a reality
13	販売している、購入できる	available for purchase *13

*9 同 establish
*13 「購入のために手に入れることができる」が直訳。フレーズとして覚えること。

右の英語部分を隠し、左の日本語だけを見て、
英単語・フレーズを即座に言えるようにする練習です。

14	確かに～だが、…だ	it is true that ～ but ...
15	低～中価格の製品	low- to mid-range product
16	市場に出回っている	on the market
17	認識する	recognize
18	優れた品質	superior quality
19	～の価値がある	worth ～
20	～するために	in order to *do*
21	～を見る	take a look at ～
22	証言	testimony
23	～に興味を持つ	be interested in ～
24	私たちが提供するもの	what we have to offer
25	質問をとっておく	save your questions

STEP 2

Shadowing & Repeating

シャドーイング＆リピーティング

SHA 47 REP 48

Good afternoon, everyone.// My name is Ryu Kawamoto.// Thank you for attending / our presentation today.// I'd like to tell you all / about our company, ABC United.// Our company mainly manufactures automobile parts / such as water pumps, / oil pumps, brake pads / and more for home and industrial use.// Our headquarters is located in Fukuoka, Japan, / but we have branch offices / in China, Spain, Thailand and India, / and we are currently working on / establishing a new factory in England.// Our company was founded about 50 years ago / by our former president, Yuki Takashima, / who was a big fan of / all things car-related.// His dream was to be able to provide / high-quality auto parts / at affordable prices.// We believe that / now, this year, / his dream has become a reality, / as our auto parts are currently available for purchase / in seven countries around the world.// It is true / that our products cost a little more / than other low- to mid-

range products / on the market, / but we believe / that our customers recognize / that the superior quality we offer / is more than worth it.// *1 In the future, / we would like to expand / into the market in this country, / and maybe even establish / a new branch of our company here.// In order to do this, / we would like to invite you all / to take a look at / some of the products we offer, / hear testimonies / from some of our satisfied customers / from around the world, / and let us know / if you are interested in / what we have to offer.// *2 Please save all of your questions / until the end of our presentation.//

＊1　... more than worth it. は、「価格以上のもの」という時の決まり文句。
＊2　... what we have to offer. は、直訳すると「私たちが提供するために持っているもの」。ここでは、have to ～ は「しなければならない」ではなく、「～するために持っている」。We have something to offer. の something が関係代名詞 what になって前に出た、と考えるとよい。

STEP 3 Sight Translation

サイト・トランスレーション

1 みなさん、こんにちは。川本リュウといいます。本日は弊社のプレゼンにご出席頂きありがとうございます。これから弊社 ABC United について皆様にお話ししたいと思います。

2 弊社が主に製造しているのは自動車部品です。ウォーターポンプ、オイルポンプ、ブレーキパッドや、その他家庭用、業務用製品を（製造しております）。

3 本社は日本の福岡にありますが、中国、スペイン、タイ、インドに支社があり、現在英国に新しい工場を設立しようとしているところです。

4 弊社は約 50 年前に前社長、高島裕樹が設立しました。高島は自動車関連のすべてのものが大好きでした。彼の夢は、高品質の自動車部品を手ごろな価格で提供することでした。

5 そして今年、彼の夢が現実になったと思っています。弊社の自動車部品は現在世界 7 カ国で販売されているからです。

6 弊社製品は確かに、市場に出回っている他社の低～中価格製品よりも、値段は少し高いのですが、お客様に納得して頂けると信じています、弊社の提供する優れた品質は価格以上のものだと。

7 将来、弊社はこの国の市場に進出し、できればこちらに新しい支社を設立したいと考えています。

8 そのためには、みなさまに弊社製品の一部を見て頂き、世界中の満足したお客様の声（←証言）を聞いて頂きたいと思います。そして弊社製品（←提供するために私たちが持っているもの）に興味を持たれましたら、私どもにお知らせください。プレゼン終了後に質問をお受けします（←プレゼン終了後まで質問はお待ちください）。

右の英語を隠し、左の日本語を見ながら、
前からどんどん英語で言う練習です。

1 Good afternoon, everyone. My name is Ryu Kawamoto. Thank you for attending our presentation today. I'd like to tell you all about our company, ABC United.

2 Our company mainly manufactures automobile parts such as water pumps, oil pumps, brake pads and more for home and industrial use.

3 Our headquarters is located in Fukuoka, Japan, but we have branch offices in China, Spain, Thailand and India, and we are currently working on establishing a new factory in England.

4 Our company was founded about 50 years ago by our former president, Yuki Takashima, who was a big fan of all things car-related. His dream was to be able to provide high-quality auto parts at affordable prices.

5 We believe that now, this year, his dream has become a reality, as our auto parts are currently available for purchase in seven countries around the world.

6 It is true that our products cost a little more than other low- to mid-range products on the market, but we believe that our customers recognize that the superior quality we offer is more than worth it.

7 In the future, we would like to expand into the market in this country, and maybe even establish a new branch of our company here.

8 In order to do this, we would like to invite you all to take a look at some of the products we offer, hear testimonies from some of our satisfied customers from around the world, and let us know if you are interested in what we have to offer. Please save all of your questions until the end of our presentation.

STEP 4

Reproduction

イラストを見てリプロダクション

1

2

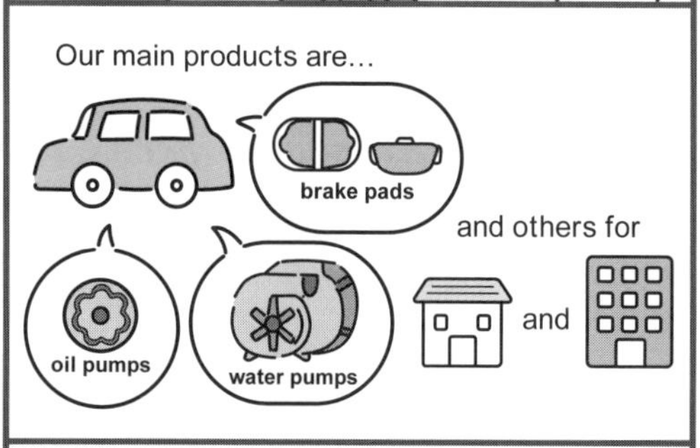

3

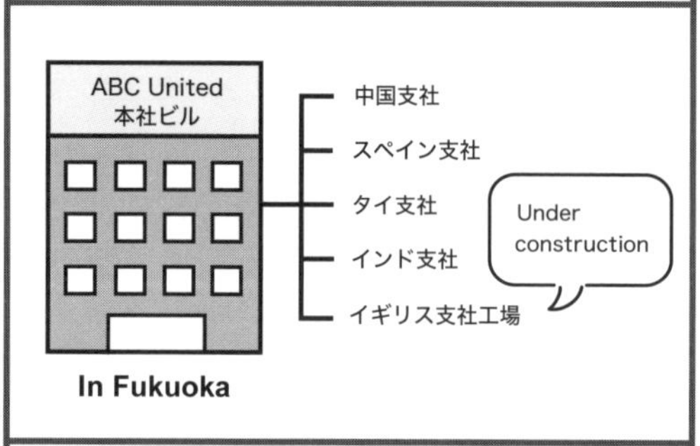

4

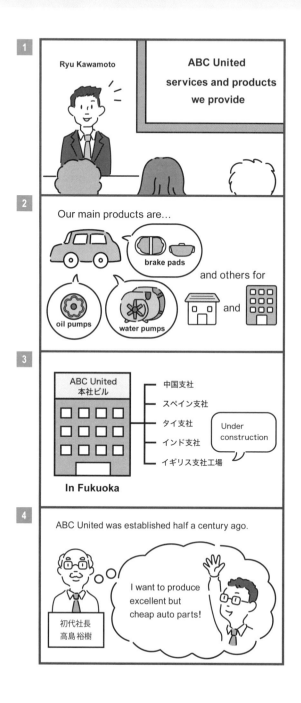

イラストを見ながら、英語で説明してみましょう。

5

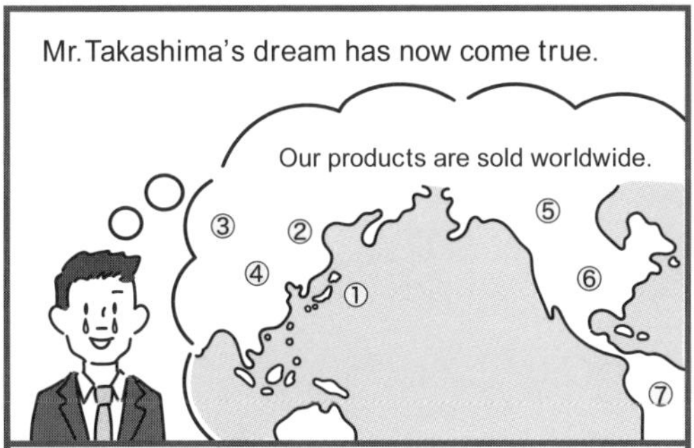

6

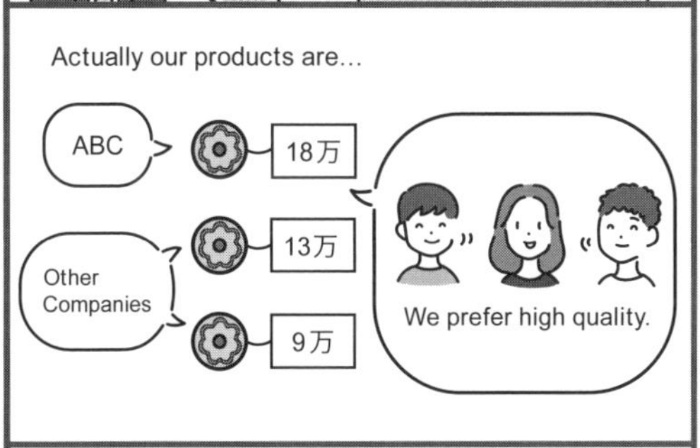

7

8

Lesson 17

Company introduction Part 2

Talking about company structure

会社紹介 2

社内組織と構造の紹介

STEP 1

Quick Response

クイック・レスポンス

49

01	簡単に説明する	briefly explain
02	内部の事情、内部構造	inner workings
03	経営する、業務を行う	run operations
04	独立して	independently
05	～に報告する	report to ～
06	本社	head office
07	～に分けられる	be divided into ～
08	(人や仕事を) 監督する	oversee
09	部長、室長、GM	general manager *9
10	課長、マネージャー	manager *10
11	課長補佐、アシスタント・マネージャー	assistant manager *11
12	品質管理	quality control
13	～以外の	other than ～

*9, 10, 11 ここでは「部長」「課長」「課長補佐」という代表的な訳語を当てたが、会社によって訳語は違うので注意。

右の英語部分を隠し、左の日本語だけを見て、
英単語・フレーズを即座に言えるようにする練習です。

14	～を…に任せる	leave ～ to ...
15	会社の経営	company management
16	～のおかげで	thanks to ～
17	海外展開、国際的事業展開	global presence
18	組織体制、組織構成	organizational structure
19	～を現地生産する	produce ～ locally
20	資源	resources
21	～を同じ基準に保つ	hold ～ to the same standard
22	厳しい	rigorous
23	維持する	maintain
24	仕入れ先、サプライヤー	supplier
25	生産設備	production equipment
26	保証する、確保する	ensure
27	均一に保つ、常に一貫する	stay consistent

I would now like to briefly explain / the inner workings of our company.// Each of our companies abroad / runs operations independently, / and they report to our head office in Japan / at least once a week.// Each company is divided / into office staff and factory staff.// The factory is overseen / by a general manager.// Under this GM, / there are a manager and an assistant manager / for each department: / quality control, / production, shipping, and so on.// Other than that, / we leave the details of company management / to each of our branches.// Thanks to our global presence / and strong organizational structure, / we can provide our high quality products / to people in many different countries.// As I mentioned, / each of our overseas branches / operates its own factory, / so we are able to / produce our parts locally, /*1 using

＊1　なお「現地調達する」は procure ～ locally という。「現地生産する」とペアで覚えておきたい。「現地調達」なら local procurement。(例) locally procured parts (現地調達した部品)

materials and resources from the area.// We hold our quality of production / in our overseas branches / to the same rigorous standards / that we maintain in Japan.// We allow each branch / to find their own suppliers for materials, / but all of the basic production equipment / in our factories / is made in Japan.// This is to ensure / that production quality stays consistent / at all of our facilities.// If you have any questions, / please feel free to ask now.//

STEP 3 Sight Translation

サイト・トランスレーション

1 では、弊社の内部（事情）について手短にお話ししたいと思います。弊社の海外支社は、それぞれ独立して業務を行っており、少なくとも週に１回、日本の本社に報告をします。

2 各支社は事務職員とファクトリー・スタッフで構成されています。工場はGMが監督者（統括責任者）です。このGMのもとにマネージャー、アシスタント・マネージャーがいます。品質管理、製造、発送などの部署ごとに。

3 それ以外の、会社管理の詳細は、各支社に任せています。

4 海外展開と強固な組織体制のおかげで、弊社は多くのさまざまな国の人々に高品質の製品を販売することができるのです。

5 いまお話ししましたように、各海外支社は独自の工場運営をしており、部品の現地生産が可能です、材料と資源を現地調達して。

6 海外支社の生産品質は、日本と同じ厳しい基準を保持しています。

7 私どもは、各支社に、サプライヤー（材料の仕入れ先）の選定を独自に行わせていますが、工場の基本的な生産設備はすべて、日本製です。こうすることで、すべての工場で、製品の品質を均一に保つことができるのです。

8 質問のある方は、ご自由にお尋ねください。

右の英語を隠し、左の日本語を見ながら、
前からどんどん英語で言う練習です。

1 I would now like to briefly explain the inner workings of our company. Each of our companies abroad runs operations independently, and they report to our head office in Japan at least once a week.

2 Each company is divided into office staff and factory staff. The factory is overseen by a general manager. Under this GM, there are a manager and an assistant manager for each department: quality control, production, shipping, and so on.

3 Other than that, we leave the details of company management to each of our branches.

4 Thanks to our global presence and strong organizational structure, we can provide our high-quality products to people in many different countries.

5 As I mentioned, each of our overseas branches operates its own factory, so we are able to produce our parts locally, using materials and resources from the area.

6 We hold our quality of production in our overseas branches to the same rigorous standards that we maintain in Japan.

7 We allow each branch to find their own suppliers for materials, but all of the basic production equipment in our factories is made in Japan. This is to ensure that production quality stays consistent at all of our facilities.

8 If you have any questions, please feel free to ask now.

STEP 4 Reproduction

イラストを見てリプロダクション

1

2

3

We entrust the management to each branch.

4

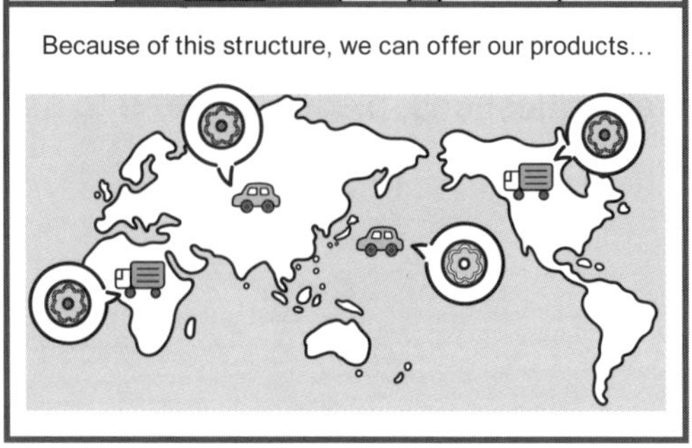

Because of this structure, we can offer our products...

イラストを見ながら、英語で説明してみましょう。

5

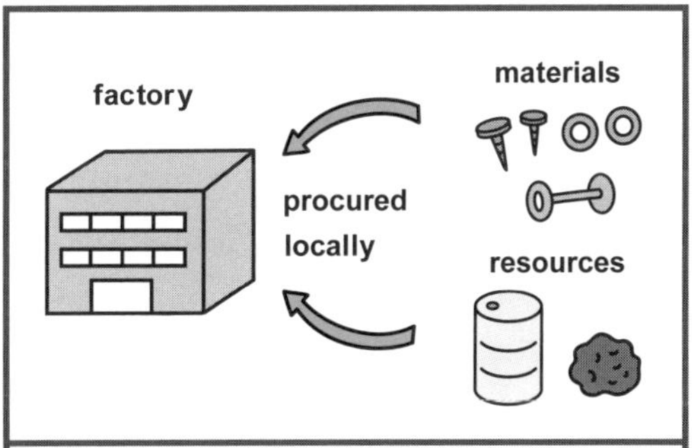

6

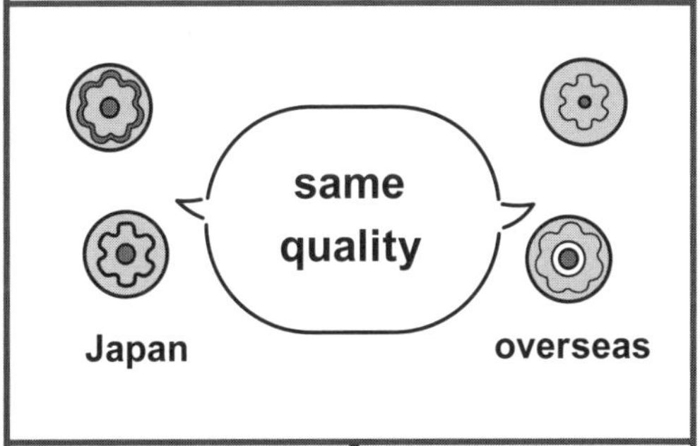

7

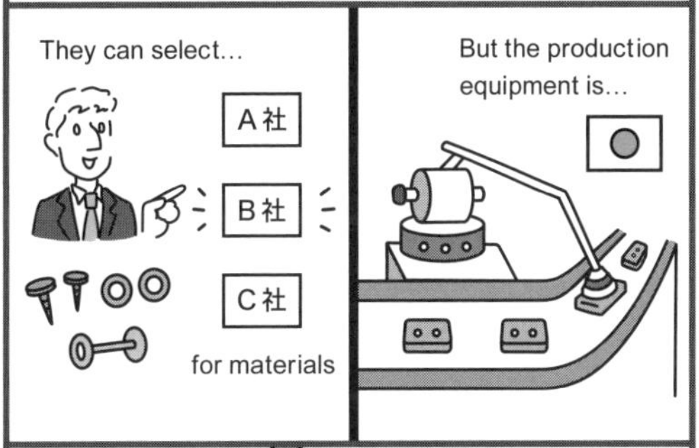

8

Lesson 18

Culture shock seminar Part 1

The Japanese employment system

カルチャーショックセミナー 1

日本の雇用形態

STEP 1 Quick Response

クイック・レスポンス

52

01	おおまかな枠組み	general framework
02	雇用	employment
03	終身雇用制	lifetime employment system
04	年功序列賃金制度	seniority-based wage system
05	廃れる、消えていく	fade out of style
06	使用されている	be in use
07	利点、手当	benefit *7
08	絶対的な	absolute
09	雇用保障	job security
10	今度は、その結果として	in turn
11	(人)に~する意欲を沸かせる	motivate someone to *do*
12	~に忠実である	be loyal to ~
13	彼らのニーズにぴったり適合する	fit their exact need
14	昇進	promotion

*7 「手当、給付金、福利厚生」の意味で用いられるときは、benefits と複数形になるのが普通。
(例) A person who worked for at least ten years is eligible for retirement benefits.
(10 年以上働いた人は、退職金を受ける資格がある)

右の英語部分を隠し、左の日本語だけを見て、
英単語・フレーズを即座に言えるようにする練習です。

15	勤続年数、在職期間	length of service
16	～に移行する、変わる	switch to ～
17	能力給制度	merit-based pay system
18	～に限定される	be limited to ～
19	ベンチャー企業、新興企業	start-up company
20	資産運用会社	asset management company
21	組織の	organizational
22	意思決定	decision-making
23	～の核心にある、 ～の最重要部分である	be at the heart of ～
24	結果として	as a result
25	個人（の）、個々（の）	individual
26	業績、成果	accomplishment
27	通例、慣例	common practice
28	賃金	wage

Let me explain / the general framework of employment / here in Japan.// Two of the biggest differences / between Japanese companies and Western companies / are Japan's lifetime employment system / and seniority-based wage system.// These systems are slowly fading out of style, / but they are still in use / in major companies.// Some of the benefits / of the lifetime employment system / are that employees receive absolute job security / and benefits for their family, / which in turn motivates them / to work harder for / and be more loyal to the company.// It also allows companies / to train employees / to fit their exact need / and keep them long-term.// Next, I'd like to explain / the seniority-based wage system.// It is a system / where promotions are based on / length of service and age.// The longer you work at a company,

/ the more your salary increases.// *1 Also, bonuses are given / twice a year.// Recently, some companies have switched / to a merit-based pay system, / but this is limited to / just a few start-up / and asset management companies.// One reason / the seniority-based wage system / has been in wide use for so long / is that group or organizational decision-making / is at the heart of Japanese business.// Different from the top-down system of the West, / Japanese companies usually use / a bottom-up method / to make decisions.// As a result, / as it is difficult to judge / each individual's accomplishments, / it is common practice / to increase all wages equally.//

＊1 The longer you work at a company, the more your salary increases. the + 比較級, the + 比較級は、「～すればするほど、ますます…」。(例) "When do you need this ?"– "The sooner, the better." (「いつこれが必要ですか?」–「早ければ早いほどいいです」)

STEP 3

Sight Translation

サイト・トランスレーション

1 ここ日本における雇用の大枠について説明させてください。日本企業と西洋の企業の間の2つの大きな違いは、日本には終身雇用制と年功序列賃金制度があるということです。

2 これらの制度は徐々に廃れてはいるものの、大企業ではいまだに使われています。

3 終身雇用制の利点は、社員は絶対的な雇用保障と家族手当（扶養手当）を受けられることです。これにより、社員はさらに会社のために働く意欲が湧き、会社により忠実となります。

4 また、会社側も、（会社の）必要に応じて社員を訓練し、彼らを長期にわたって確保（雇用）することができます。

5 次に、年功序列賃金制度について説明します。これは昇進が勤続年数や年齢に応じて行われる制度です。会社に長く勤めるほど、給料が上がります。また、賞与も年2回支給されます。

6 最近では能力給に移行する企業もありますが、それは、一部のベンチャー企業や資産運用会社に限られています。

7 年功序列賃金制度が、長い間、広く採用されてきた理由のひとつは、グループ・組織単位での意思決定が日本式ビジネスの核心にあるからです（最重要部分だからです）。

8 西洋のトップダウン方式とは違い、日本の企業はたいていボトムアップ方式で意思決定をします。結果として個人の成果を判断しにくいため、全体の賃金を均一に上げていくのが通例となっているのです。

右の英語を隠し、左の日本語を見ながら、
前からどんどん英語で言う練習です。

1 Let me explain the general framework of employment here in Japan. Two of the biggest differences between Japanese companies and Western companies are Japan's lifetime employment system and seniority-based wage system.

2 These systems are slowly fading out of style, but they are still in use in major companies.

3 Some of the benefits of the lifetime employment system are that employees receive absolute job security and benefits for their family, which in turn motivates them to work harder for and be more loyal to the company.

4 It also allows companies to train employees to fit their exact need and keep them long-term.

5 Next, I'd like to explain the seniority-based wage system. It is a system where promotions are based on length of service and age. The longer you work at a company, the more your salary increases. Also, bonuses are given twice a year.

6 Recently, some companies have switched to a merit-based pay system, but this is limited to just a few start-up and asset management companies.

7 One reason the seniority-based wage system has been in wide use for so long is that group or organizational decision-making is at the heart of Japanese business.

8 Different from the top-down system of the West, Japanese companies usually use a bottom-up method to make decisions. As a result, as it is difficult to judge each individual's accomplishments, it is common practice to increase all wages equally.

STEP 4 Reproduction

イラストを見てリプロダクション

1

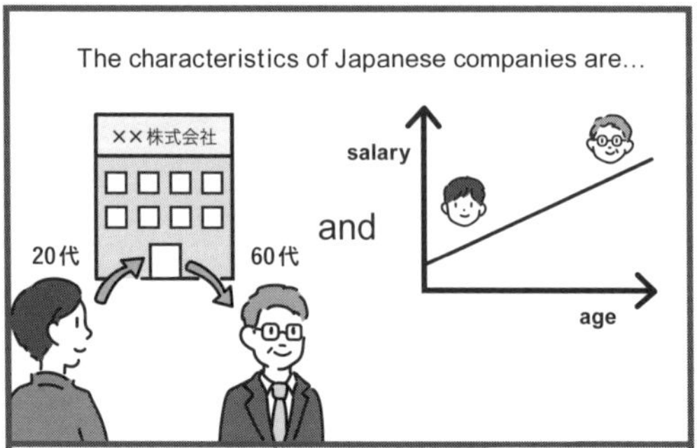

2

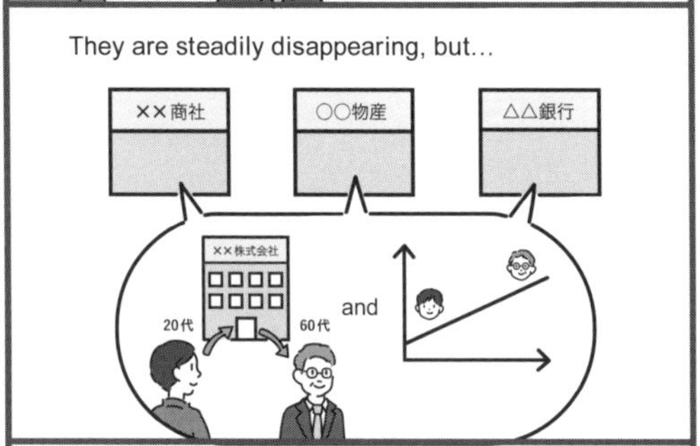

3

4

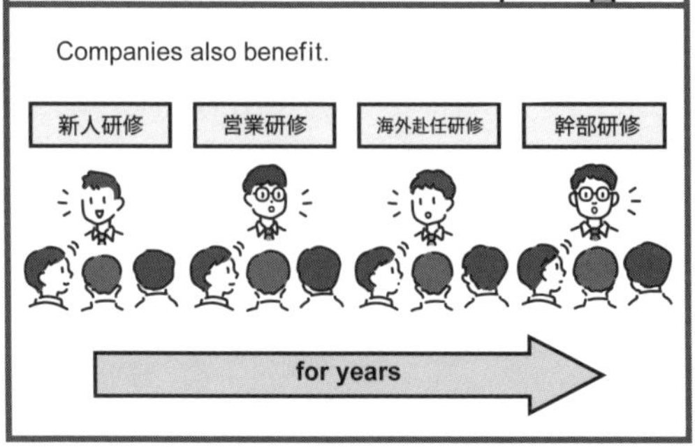

イラストを見ながら、英語で説明してみましょう。

5

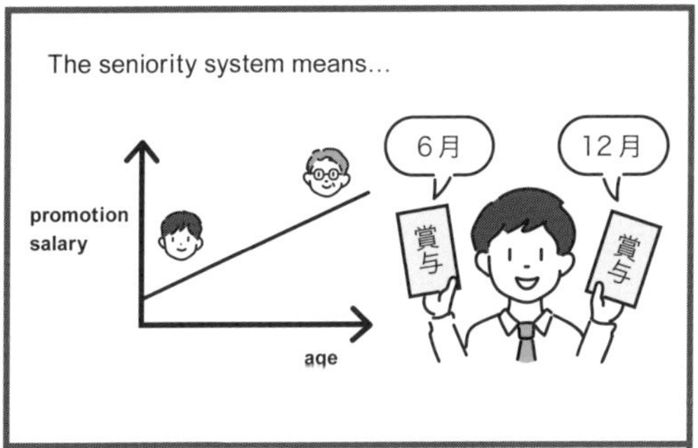

6

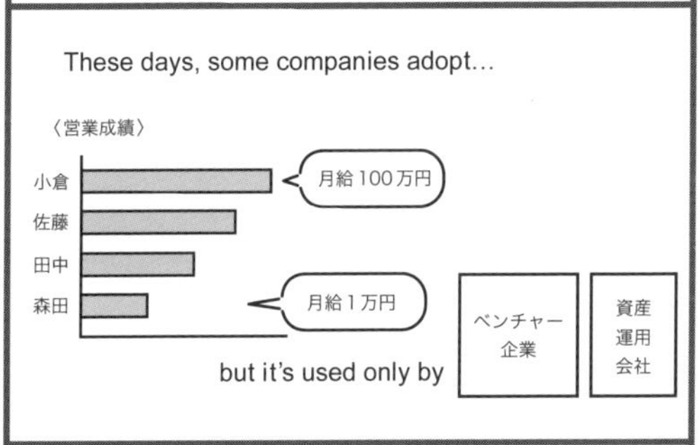

but it's used only by

7

Why has the seniority system been so popular?

8

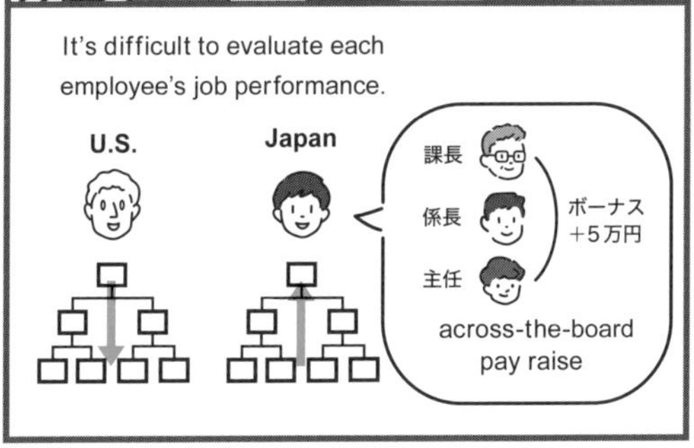

It's difficult to evaluate each employee's job performance.

across-the-board pay raise

Lesson 19

Culture shock seminar Part 2

Japanese work flow

カルチャーショックセミナー 2

日本的な仕事の進め方

STEP 1

Quick Response

クイック・レスポンス　55

01

～に注意する　be careful about ～

02

～を心に留めておく、覚えておく　keep ～ in mind

03

運営する　operate

04

ボトムアップベースで　on a bottom-up basis ＊4

05

従業員、社員　employee ＊5

06

（権利など）を行使する　exercise

07

会議が開かれる　a meeting is held

08

頻繁に　frequently

09

会社全体のコンセンサス　company-wide consensus

10

～する傾向にある　tend to *do*

11

仕事関連のこと　work-related matters

12

飲み会　drinking party

13

延々と続く、長引く　drag on

＊4 on a ～ basis は「～基準で、単位で」という熟語。（例）Applications will be accepted on a first-come, first-served basis.（申し込みは先着順で受け付けます）

＊5 employer なら「雇用者」。cf. employ「雇う、雇用する」、employment「雇用」

右の英語部分を隠し、左の日本語だけを見て、
英単語・フレーズを即座に言えるようにする練習です。

14	結論に至る、結論を出す	come to a conclusion
15	～することを意図されている、 ～することが目的である	be meant to *do* ＊15
16	一貫して	consistently
17	徹底的に話し合う	talk ～ out
18	我々のチームワークを築く	build our teamwork
19	～に結びつく	tie into ～
20	無駄に、効果なく	in vain
21	（人）に～を知らせる	inform someone of ～
22	同僚	colleague
23	～のことを言う、言及する	refer to ～
24	プロジェクトの日々の進捗状況	daily progress of a project
25	先輩、年長者	senior
26	詳細な情報	detailed information
27	～と結びついている	be tied with ～

＊15 同 be intended to *do*

STEP 2

Shadowing & Repeating

シャドーイング＆リピーティング

SHA 56 REP 57

There are a few things / you should be careful about.// Keep in mind / that things are done a little differently here / than in Western companies.// Since Japanese companies operate / on a bottom-up basis, / most employees do not exercise / any individual right to make decisions.// Instead, meetings are held / much more frequently / in order to ensure company-wide consensus.// It may surprise you to find / that we tend to often continue / to talk about work-related matters / even after we have left the office, / like at drinking parties.// Sometimes meetings may drag on for a long time, / and they may not come to a clear conclusion.// Many meetings aren't meant / to have any set conclusion.// But by consistently talking things out, / we are able to build our teamwork, / which all ties into the success of our projects.// So there is no need to worry / that this is all done in vain.// There is a uniquely Japanese system / called *Ho-ren-so*.// Let me explain a little about the *Ho-ren-so*, / or "report, contact and consult" system.// It is a system / where you make sure / to inform your supervisor or colleagues / of your progress at each step / of the process of a project.// "Report" refers mainly / to reporting your progress and results / to your supervisor.// "Contact" means / sharing the daily progress of a project / with the rest of your team members, / including your seniors.// And you "consult" with them / to improve on the project.//*1 This is repeated over and over / until the project is done.// We believe / that sharing such detailed information / among the group / is also tied with teamwork and success.//

*1 ... to improve on the project の improve on ～ は、「～をより良いものにする、より良い成果を挙げる」の意味。（例）We appreciate the feedback and will continue to improve on the product.（ご意見ありがとうございます。これからも製品をより良いものにしていく所存です）

STEP 3

Sight Translation

サイト・トランスレーション

1 皆さんが注意しておいたほうがいいことがいくつかあります。西洋の企業と、ここ（日本）では少しやり方が違うということを覚えておいてください。日本企業はボトムアップベースで運営されているので、ほとんどの社員は個人的な決定権を行使することはありません。

2 その代わり、会社全体のコンセンサスを取るために、（西洋企業に比べて）会議がかなり頻繁に開かれます。皆さん驚くかもしれませんが、仕事関連の話を続けることが多いのです、会社を出た後の飲み会などでも。

3 時には会議が長時間にわたり、しかも明確な結論が出ないかもしれません。会議の多くはきちんとした結論を出すことを目的としていません。

4 ですが一貫して徹底的に話し合うことで、チームワークを築くことができ、それがすべて私たちのプロジェクトの成功に結びつくのです。ですから（会議で結論が出なくて）全く無駄だったと心配する必要はありません。

5 ホウレンソウという日本独自のシステムがあります。ホウレンソウ—報告、連絡、相談—について、少し説明しましょう。これは、上司や同僚に、プロジェクト進行のステップごとに必ず進捗状況を知らせる、というシステムです。

6 「報告」は、主に仕事の経過や結果を上司に報告することを意味します。「連絡」は、プロジェクトの日々の進捗状況を共有することを意味します、先輩（上司）を含めたチームメンバーと。

7 そして彼らと「相談」をし、プロジェクトを改善していきます。プロジェクトが終わるまで、これが何度も繰り返されるのです。

8 グループ内でこうした詳細な情報を共有することも、チームワーク（とプロジェクト）の成功につながると私たちは信じています。

右の英語を隠し、左の日本語を見ながら、
前からどんどん英語で言う練習です。

1 There are a few things you should be careful about. Keep in mind that things are done a little differently here than in Western companies. Since Japanese companies operate on a bottom-up basis, most employees do not exercise any individual right to make decisions.

2 Instead, meetings are held much more frequently in order to ensure company-wide consensus. It may surprise you to find that we tend to often continue to talk about work-related matters even after we have left the office, like at drinking parties.

3 Sometimes meetings may drag on for a long time, and they may not come to a clear conclusion. Many meetings aren't meant to have any set conclusion.

4 But by consistently talking things out, we are able to build our teamwork, which all ties into the success of our projects. So there is no need to worry that this is all done in vain.

5 There is a uniquely Japanese system called *Ho-ren-so*. Let me explain a little about the *Ho-ren-so*, or "report, contact and consult" system. It is a system where you make sure to inform your supervisor or colleagues of your progress at each step of the process of a project.

6 "Report" refers mainly to reporting your progress and results to your supervisor. "Contact" means sharing the daily progress of a project with the rest of your team members, including your seniors.

7 And you "consult" with them to improve on the project. This is repeated over and over until the project is done.

8 We believe that sharing such detailed information among the group is also tied with teamwork and success.

STEP 4 Reproduction

イラストを見てリプロダクション

1

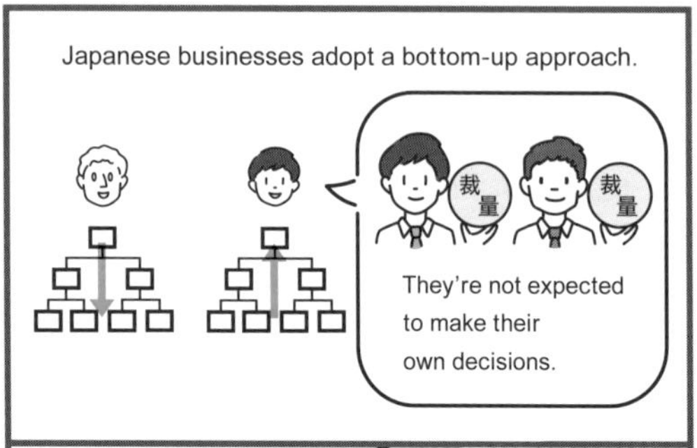

2

3

4

イラストを見ながら、英語で説明してみましょう。

5

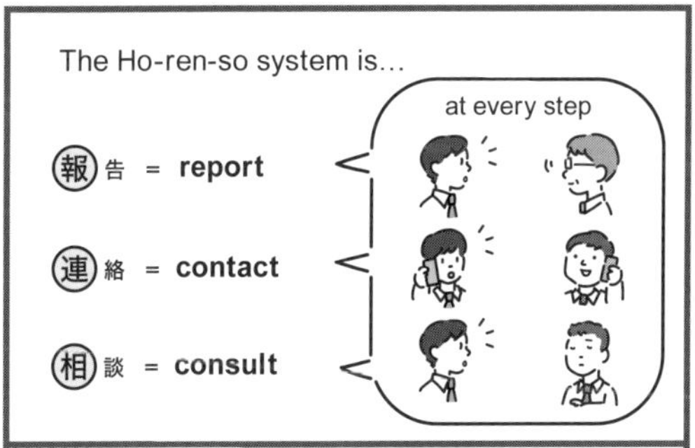

6

7

8

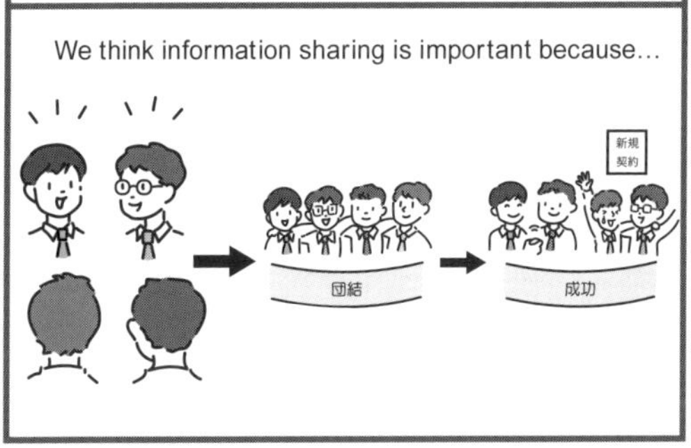

Lesson 20

Culture shock seminar Part 3

Explaining paid time off and health care

カルチャーショックセミナー 3

有給休暇取得と保険の説明

STEP 1

Quick Response

クイック・レスポンス

58

01	日本企業	Japanese businesses
02	有給休暇	paid leave
03	～をよく知る、熟知する	get familiar with ～
04	国民の祝日	national holiday
05	正月休み	New Year holiday
06	もし～の場合には	in the event that ～*6
07	有休をとる	take time off from work with pay *7
08	書類に記入する	fill out the form
09	有給休暇	paid vacation
10	直属の上司	immediate supervisor
11	承認をもらう	receive approval
12	～を…に正式に提出する	file ～ with ...
13	人事部	personnel department

＊6　in the event that ～ = if ～「もし～ならば」
＊7　with pay は「給料をもらって」。直訳すると「給料をもらって仕事を休む」。

右の英語部分を隠し、左の日本語だけを見て、
英単語・フレーズを即座に言えるようにする練習です。

14	～を受ける資格・権利がある	be entitled to ～
15	法的に	legally
16	銀行口座	bank account
17	一括で、まとめて	in one lump sum *17
18	税金	tax
19	保険料	insurance premium
20	自動的に差し引かれる	be automatically deducted
21	給料（小切手）	paycheck *21
22	健康保険証	health insurance card
23	忘れずに～する	remember to *do*
24	書類	paperwork
25	内部の	internal
26	医療記録	medical record

＊17 反 in installments 分割払いで
＊21 check は「小切手」だが、paycheck は salary, wage の意味で使われる。

As you may already know, / Japanese businesses handle paid leave / differently from Western companies.// First, it would be a good idea / to get a Japanese calendar / and get familiar with / all of the 15 national holidays.//*1 We usually have / our bigger breaks of the year / in the spring, summer and around the New Year holiday.// In the event / that you would like to take time off / from work with pay, / you need to first fill out / a paid vacation request form / and send it to your immediate supervisor.// After you receive approval / from your supervisor, / you have to file your request / with the personnel department.// Requests must be filed / at least one week before / the day you plan to take off.// In addition to the 15 national holidays, / we are legally entitled to / at least 10 paid vacation days per year.// Now, concerning your salary, / it will

＊1　現在は年間 16 日の国民の祝日がある。

英語の音声を聞きながら口まねする練習と、
英語の音声のあとのポーズで英文を発声してみる練習です。

be transferred to your bank account / in one lump sum / on the 25th of each month.// Taxes and insurance premiums / will be automatically deducted / from your paycheck.// We get bonuses twice a year / in June and December.// I believe / you should have already received /[*2] your company health insurance card.// You can use that / whenever you go to a doctor's office or the hospital, / but please remember / to save any paperwork you receive / while you are there.// You may need it / for our internal medical records later.//

＊2 ... you should have already received ... should + have + *done* は「〜したはずだ」。
(例) He should have arrived in London by now.（今頃、彼はロンドンに着いているはずだ）

STEP 3 Sight Translation

サイト・トランスレーション

1 もうご存知かもしれませんが、日本企業では西洋の企業とは違ったやり方で有給休暇を扱います。まず、日本のカレンダーを手にいれて、15 の祝日すべてを知っておくのがいいでしょう。

2 日本ではたいてい、春、夏、そしてお正月の前後に長めの休暇を取ります。

3 有給休暇を取りたいときには、まずは有給休暇申請書に記入し、直属の上司に送る必要があります。上司から許可をもらったら、その書類を人事課に提出しなくてはなりません。

4 申請は、休暇予定日の少なくとも 1 週間前に提出しなければなりません。15 日の祝日に加え、有給休暇は法的に少なくとも年間 10 日もらう権利があります。

5 次に、給料についてですが、給与は毎月 25 日に、みなさんの銀行口座に一括振り込みされます。税金と保険料は、みなさんの給料から自動的に差し引かれます。

6 ボーナスは年に 2 回、6 月と 12 月にもらえます。

7 みなさん、もう会社支給の保険証は受け取ったはずですね。医院や病院に行くときにはいつも必要です（←使うことができます）。

8 ですが、そこで受け取った書類は必ず保管しておいてください。あとで内部の医療記録のために必要になるかもしれないからです。

右の英語を隠し、左の日本語を見ながら、
前からどんどん英語で言う練習です。

1 As you may already know, Japanese businesses handle paid leave differently from Western companies. First, it would be a good idea to get a Japanese calendar and get familiar with all of the 15 national holidays.

2 We usually have our bigger breaks of the year in the spring, summer and around the New Year holiday.

3 In the event that you would like to take time off from work with pay, you need to first fill out a paid vacation request form and send it to your immediate supervisor. After you receive approval from your supervisor, you have to file your request with the personnel department.

4 Requests must be filed at least one week before the day you plan to take off. In addition to the 15 national holidays, we are legally entitled to at least 10 paid vacation days per year.

5 Now, concerning your salary, it will be transferred to your bank account in one lump sum on the 25th of each month. Taxes and insurance premiums will be automatically deducted from your paycheck.

6 We get bonuses twice a year in June and December.

7 I believe you should have already received your company health insurance card. You can use that whenever you go to a doctor's office or the hospital,

8 but please remember to save any paperwork you receive while you are there. You may need it for our internal medical records later.

STEP 4

Reproduction

イラストを見てリプロダクション

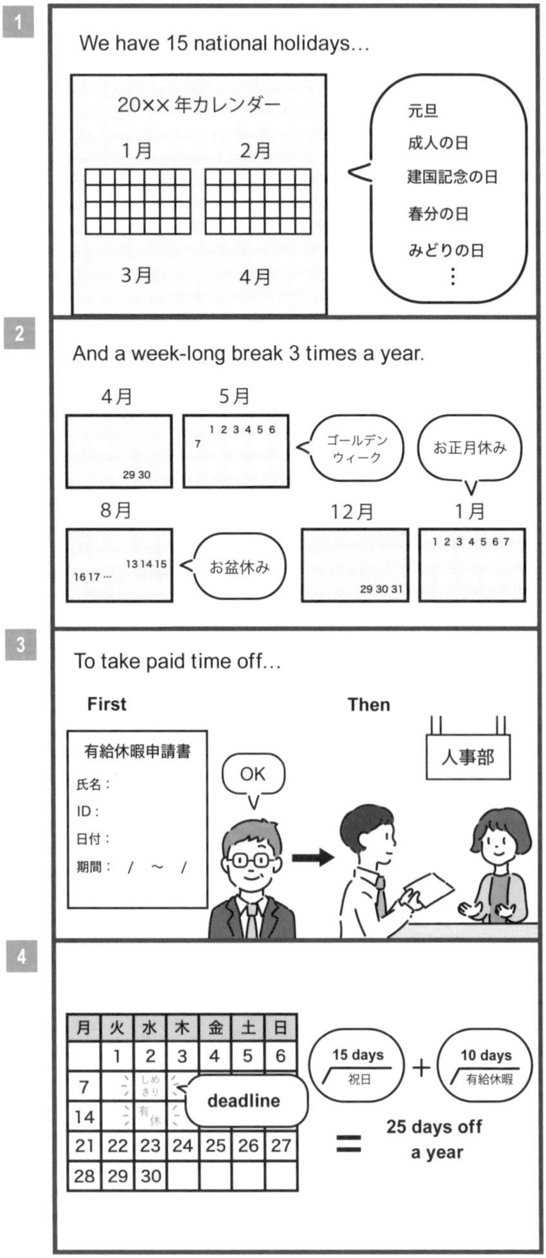

イラストを見ながら、英語で説明してみましょう。

5

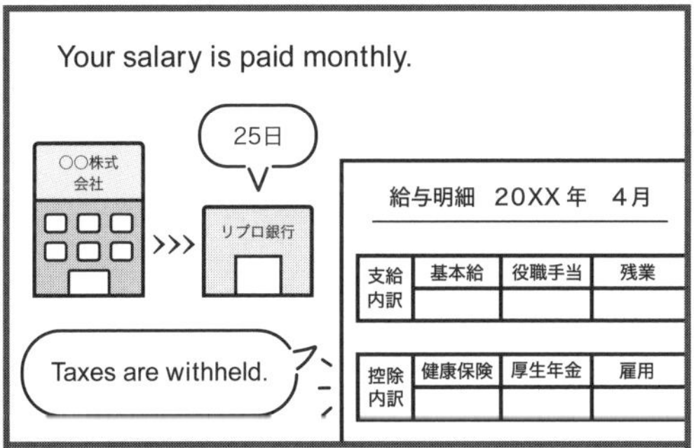

6

7

8

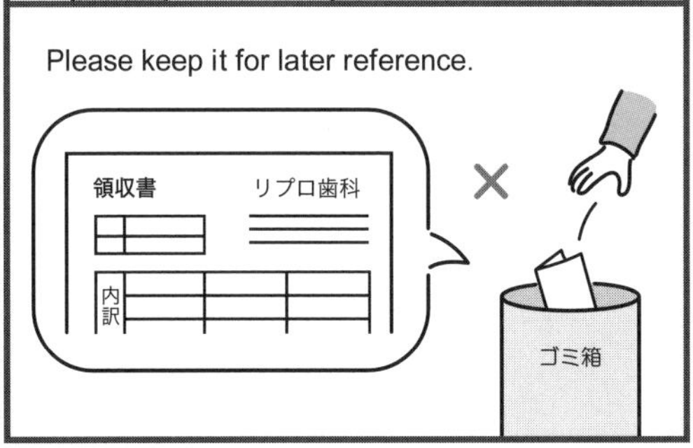

著者紹介

小倉　慶郎（Yoshiro Ogura）

東京都生まれ。学習院大学大学院イギリス文学専攻博士前期課程修了。通訳者・翻訳家、インタースクール大阪校講師などを経て、現在は、大阪公立大学国際基幹教育機構　教授。専門は、英語教育、通訳・翻訳論、異文化コミュニケーション、ジャーナリズム。主な通訳業績として「日英高等教育シンポジウム」、「国際環境フォーラム」。翻訳書に『静かなる戦争』（ハルバースタム、PHP 研究所）、『奇跡の人 ヘレンケラー自伝』（新潮文庫）。著書に『BBC WORLD 英語リスニング サイトトランスレーション』、『BBC WORLD 英語リスニング UK ニュース入門』（共に DHC）、『東大英語長文が 5 分で読めるようになる』（語学春秋社）などがある。日本英語コミュニケーション学会理事。文部科学省指定・英語教育改善のための調査研究事業運営指導員（大阪府立泉陽高等学校）。大阪府内の高等学校では、「通訳訓練法を使った英語学習」「英日通訳入門」などの出張講義を随時行っている。

英語リプロダクショントレーニング
ビジネス編　改訂新版

[PRODUCTION STAFF]

装丁　Pesco Paint（清水裕久）

DTP　Pesco Paint

イラスト　HACHH

© Yoshiro Ogura 2024 Printed in Japan

本書の無断転載、複製、複写（コピー）、翻訳を禁じます。

本書を代行業者等の第三者に依頼してスキャンやデジタル化することは、たとえ個人や家庭内の利用であっても、著作権法上、認められておりません。

学研グループの書籍・雑誌についての新刊情報・詳細情報は、下記をご覧ください。

学研出版サイト　https://hon.gakken.jp/